THE MAN OF BUSINESS

THE MAN OF BUSINESS

His Influence, Temptations, Responsibilities,

Enterprise and Principles of Action

JAMES W. ALEXANDER

WILLIAM B. SPRAGUE

JOHN TODD

STEPHEN H. TYNG

ISAAC FERRIS

JONATHAN F. STEARNS

SOLID GROUND CHRISTIAN BOOKS
BIRMINGHAM, ALABAMA USA

Solid Ground Christian Books
2090 Columbiana Rd, Suite 2000
Birmingham, AL 35216
205-443-0311
sgcb@charter.net
http://solid-ground-books.com

The Man of Business
His Influence, Temptations, Responsibilities,
Enterprise and Principles of Action

James W. Alexander (1804-1859)
William B. Sprague (1795-1876)
John Todd (1800-1873)
Stephen H. Tyng (1800-1885)
Isaac Ferris (1798-1873)
Jonathan F. Stearns (1808-1889)

Solid Ground Classic Reprints

First printing of new edition July 2005

Taken from 1864 edition by William P. Nimmo, Edinburgh

Cover work by Borgo Design, Tuscaloosa, AL
Contact them at nelbrown@comcast.net

Cover image is an old image of Wall Street, 1850.

ISBN: 1-59925-001-2

PREFACE.

THE following series of practical papers on the influence, temptations, responsibilities, enterprise, and principles of action of men of business, now reprinted in a complete form for the first time, was originally published in New York a few years ago. From the high position of the writers, comprising, as they still do, several of the most eminent clergymen of the American pulpit, and also from their very able treatment of the subjects placed in their hands to elucidate and enforce, the book at once secured a prominent position in public favour, which it still deservedly maintains.

The nature and object in view in preparing the Work are so well set forth in the original preface that the present Editor cannot better explain them than by the following extract from it:—

" Such a Work as the one now prepared for

the publisher, who has assumed the responsibility of issuing this, will, it is hoped, be one of general interest and usefulness. It will form an appropriate guide for a young man in his start in life. It will be an useful gift to a business friend at any period of his life of experiment. It will exercise an influence for the benefit of men, only limited by its own adaptation to usefulness; for the field upon which it enters is boundless, and the persons for whom it is calculated to be a guide and a friend are innumerable. It is fully believed by the publisher to be adapted, in an eminent degree, for usefulness: he thinks that no reflecting person can read the table of contents, and remark the subjects proposed, together with the character of the reverend gentlemen who have severally written upon them at his request, without a thorough conviction of the value of the Work, and the likelihood of its usefulness to those for whom it is designed."

The Editor of the present edition has long been of opinion that books of this class, carefully, suggestively, and above all practically written, are calculated to be productive of a great amount of good. They aid the mental powers in the formation of character, and exercise a great influence on those who peruse them. The present book embraces the active business of everyday life familiar to all, and shows various phases of actual existence common to all those who are engaged in business, yet apt to be overlooked, on account of their familiarity, until the mind is directed to them by the vigorous intellects that have here taken these phases in detail; and the Editor sincerely hopes that the many important valuable precepts set forth in this little volume will secure it that position in public estimation to which it is so justly entitled.

The Work has been very carefully revised and adapted for the present edition, without, however, injury to the authors or their meaning. The order of arrangement of the articles differs from that of the original work; and they are here placed in better sequence to each other than, it is thought, they appear there.

EDINBURGH, *April, 1864.*

CONTENTS.

THE

YOUNG MAN OF BUSINESS

CHEERED AND COUNSELLED.

———————◆———————

JAMES W. ALEXANDER, D.D.

THE

YOUNG MAN OF BUSINESS

CHEERED AND COUNSELLED.

THERE is no coming back to correct the errors of
youth; as Plato reports Heraclitus to have said, no
man ever bathes twice in the same river: all things
are in rapid flow, and what is to be done for character
should be done quickly. In our hurrying age boys
become men by a sort of start or explosive advance.
Impressions upon society must therefore be made
upon youth, and if we would have good merchants we
must first have good clerks.*

Of the countless throng of city clerks some are
living under the parental roof, but the great majority
have come from the country. An invisible force bears
the youth of rural districts towards the great emporium.
While this infusion of fresh blood into the old veins is
useful in many ways to the receiving party, it involves
losses and exposures on the part of those who come.
Each of them has left a beloved circle, which, alas! he

---

* In America it is customary to denominate as "clerks" all young
men engaged in commercial pursuits, whether engaged as clerks proper,
warehousemen, salesmen, or in any other capacity. Of course, the
term is not applied to those engaged in mechanical trades.

has not yet learned to prize, and has entered into a comparatively homeless state.   Many a man of business can look back to this juncture, when he sallied into the great world alone, and he shudders at the pitfalls and precipices which he has escaped.   " Well do I remember, even at this distance from the time," says a celebrated writer, " the scene which my own home presented when I finally quitted it to embark on life's stormy and dangerous ocean.   My mother, one of the kindest and tenderest that ever bore that dear relationship, unable to sustain the parting, had retired to the garden; my sisters wept; my father walked silently by me to the edge of the town, where I was to take horse and ride to meet the coach that was to carry me to London; while my own heart was almost overwhelmed with emotion, under the idea that I was leaving home to encounter the anxieties, dangers, and responsibilities of a new and untried course." *

There is ground for these solicitudes.   This coast is strewed with blackened hulks and gaping timbers which went out of port flaunting with pennons.   The newly arrived boy or young man plunges into trouble and danger the hour he sets foot in the city.   All is strange and much is saddening; but he must keep down unmanly griefs, and he knows little of his worst enemies.   The single circumstance that parental care is henceforth removed, or made slight by distance, leaves him stripped of armour on a battle-field.   Thank God that many a Joseph has been led through this defenceless pilgrimage!   The evil is greater because it

* James's *Young Man from Home.*

is unseen. Yonder praying mother feels it at her aching heart; but the foolish boy is exulting in the sense of independence, and perhaps tempted to try some new pleasure to show that he is his own master. False confidence is the ruin of thousands. The temptations of such a position, especially in a city, are formidable. Most of these derive their main strength from the presence of evil companions; to this subject, therefore, let us devote a few moments.

Homely but golden is the old proverb, " Tell me the company you keep, and I will tell you what you are." The first company to which a young man really attaches himself often fixes his career. This, however, he often falls into at random, or more frequently has not decision of character to cast off when detected. Among many things which render bad company poisonous, one of the saddest is the extreme difficulty of getting rid of a deceitful friend. In the position which I occupy I am constantly observing that this or that youth is held down by the weight of evil comrades. To shake them off is a Herculean task; the ill attachment sticks like the coat of Nessus. Indeed, solitary amendment is often easier than disentangling one's self from corrupting alliance. Has my reader ever known a young man to remain virtuous in vicious society? Mark here the powerful argument for securing good companions.

Evil company is often elegant, delightful, and fascinating; and inexperience cannot escape the coils of the gilded serpent. What is greatly to be deplored is, that associates of this sort do not wait to be sought out, but make the first advances, and not unfrequently lie in wait for the new arrival. Unless the novice is on his guard against these seducers he will certainly fall. Most deadly is the poison when evil companions are under the same roof, perhaps at the same table; and it cannot be urged too seriously on young men to beware what lodging-houses they select, also at what dining-rooms and with what company they take their meals.

As I do not expect to touch upon any point which is more important, I would seriously demand for it the best consideration of every young man who may take these pages into his hand. Young men, I charge you in the name of all you hold dear, in the name of your parents, in the name of Almighty God, to break away from evil companions! Whatever it may cause of offence or loss, cut the connection. "Enter not," says the wise king, "into the path of the wicked, and go not in the way of evil men. Avoid it, pass not by it, turn from it, and pass away." Neglecting this, you will probably, almost certainly, destroy your worldly prospects,—will bear the disgraces of those who are even worse than yourselves, will lose your principles of morality and religion, and will run the risk of ruining yourselves for time and for eternity.

If bad company is thus fatal, how may a young stranger secure that which is good? The uncorrupted young man may be safely advised thus,—Be cautious at the start. Learn the character of those around you. Commit yourself slowly. Especially dread those specious persons who push themselves upon you. Call in the aid of older heads. Advise with the wisest of your employers as to the comrades who may be proper. Make bold to call upon the clergyman whose ministry you attend, and ask his counsel; my word for it, he will neither repel you nor give you any cause to regret the step. Seek associations in Church and in Sunday School; here you will find both companionship and protection. In like manner inquire for those associations which propose the protection, rescue, instruction, and entertainment of young men. Reject promptly, as you would the foulest and most noisome animal, every companion, however attractive, who speaks impurely, takes God's name in vain, violates the Lord's Day, indulges in intoxicating drinks, or in improper conduct of any kind. Blessed is he who meets with a good associate! A single example sometimes gives colour to the whole life.

Though it is never too late to seek reform, and though every reader should be exhorted to hasten back into the right path, yet honour and success are on the side of him who has not begun wrong. In morals, as in business, true prosperity comes from a fair start. The first steps in trade, the first hours in a situation, throw forward their influence. The ship is built on the model which is first laid down. The plans with which you put on your office-coat the day you enter your shop, store, counting-room, or bank, mark your direction. As the railway switch is turned, so your track will be. All which is so well known by employers that they commonly form their judgment of the entering lad before the first week is out, and find a verdict thus,—"John is dull;" or, "he is heedless;" or, "he is awkward—his fingers are all thumbs;" or, "you see he is an eye-servant;" or, "he is incurably lazy;" or, "he has all vices in one, for he lies now and will swindle hereafter." If it is the end that crowns the undertaking, it is the beginning that gives it form.

By what possibility can a young man begin business aright who has no notion what he seeks? Such, however, is the case of many. Ask young Smith, or Thomson, or Johnson,—"What have you set before you?" and he is dumb. He does not know why he has entered the place. If his views are mercenary, he might return the answer which is in many a heart, "To make money." But, my beloved and as yet uncorrupted young reader, making money is not the ultimate object of life. Do not mistake the means for the end. Money is but a subordinate means. Fix before you some pure and lofty aim, or you will assuredly become one of the grovellers. Let this be the pleasing of your Creator, Benefactor, and Saviour, and, inseparably from this, the realizing of a noble, generous, symmetrical character. Resolve, under God, to seek all the perfection of which your powers are capable; and go to that desk or that counter with a deep purpose never to flinch from a duty or commit a deliberate fault. Now, if you will lay down this book for three minutes, look steadily at what is proposed, and in reliance on Divine aid, settle your decision accordingly, it will be superfluous to prescribe petty rules for business.

Parents, employers, and senior associates will inculcate upon you the daily duties of your calling; indeed, you already know them, which may show you that the grand desideratum is not by-laws but inward principle. Nevertheless, take kindly a few disinterested counsels from one who is no longer young, but who has long cherished a warm sympathy with those who are beginning life. Under the general determination to do your duty, beware of early disgusts, whether towards persons or work. All new trials are burdensome; all beginnings are vexatious. He that ascends a ladder must take the lowest round. All who were above were once below. "If two men ride a horse, one must ride behind." To consider anything menial which belongs to the career of training is foolish. The greatest philosophers and the greatest commanders have passed through toils as humble and as galling. These hard rubs are an indispensable part of education, and it is best to have the worst first. Cheer up on cold winter mornings, when you blow your fingers as you walk briskly to the warehouse, or as you go home late at nights when press of business has detained you. Cheer up at the thought that it will make a man of you. Perhaps you remember Latin enough to quote the words in Virgil—"All this it will be sweet to remember hereafter." * Recall enough of history to think of what Roman and especially Spartan boys were accustomed to bear.

Whatever comes of it, put your shoulder to the wheel for a few months; by that time some of the rough places will have become plain. Wear the yoke gracefully. Every moment of this weariness and

* Olim meminisse juvabit.

trouble will turn out to your lasting profit, especially in regard to character. There are certain things which you will be ashamed to class among hardships. Such are early rising, which you should practise for pleasure and longevity, as well as religion; exercise in the open air, and on your feet; hard work, tending towards knowledge of business; punctuality, without which you can never attain wealth or honour; and tedious employment in affairs which secure you confidential regard. In all these temptations to discontent, let me venture an observation on life which I confess it cost me many years to comprehend. Uneasiness in the youthful mind arises from a fallacy that we may express thus,—"Work now, but rest and pleasure hereafter." Not merely the clerk, but the millionaire, thus deludes himself,—"I will bear these annoyances in view of the refreshing and luxurious respite of my hereafter." In opposition to all this, let me declare to you that these hours, or days, or years of repose, when the mighty, oppressive hand of the giant Business is given up, will be none the less sweet for your having taken a genuine satisfaction in your work as you went along. You will not make the journey better if, like famous pilgrims to Loretto, you put peas in your shoes. Form the habit of seeking pleasure in work; happiness in the duty of the hour.

The period when the young man is about coming of age is very important. Now it is, if ever, that he is most tempted to slip his neck out of the yoke, and most harassed with wishes prompted by false independence. No man can calculate the mercantile disasters arising from the preposterous wishes of young men, without experience, ability, connections, or capital, to rush into business for themselves. Wise delay in such cases is promotive of success. The number of principals is far too great in proportion. It is not every man who is formed to be a leader, and some are clearly pointed out for subordinate posts as long as they live. But as these are often the very persons who will be slowest to take the hint, let it be the maxim of all to adventure no sudden changes; to wait for undeniable indications of duty and discretion; to attempt nothing of the sort without the full approval of older heads; and above all, to play the man in regard to the unavoidable annoyances of a subaltern place.

To be successful and happy costs something. Assure yourself that if you yield to effeminate suggestions you sink. Nobly determine, at the hazard of some weariness and some chagrin, to pass contentedly through the appointed stages, and to become a thorough merchant. Consider how many a man, now great in business, came to town with all his personal effects in one bundle. Endeavour to set aside every disposition to make changes, except where they tend to moral benefit or knowledge of business. "It is ill transplanting a tree which thrives well in the soil." Let the cheerfulness of a contented mind evince itself in deference and submission to those who control your time, and in uniform good-nature and courtesy to your companions in business. With such principles and resolutions, and with reliance on Divine Providence, you may boldly hope. Brace your nerves to meet

every engagement, and, however poor, you will succeed.
Dismiss from your soul all belief in the divinity of
modern pagans, called Luck, and stake nothing on
sudden windfalls. "In human nature," says Playfair,
"there is no struggle that appears more unequal at first
sight than that of a man without connections or capital,
against the man who has both; yet there is no contest
which so constantly terminates in favour of him who
appears to have the disadvantage."

Very delicate is the situation of the young man who
is required by an employer to do that which is dishonest
or dishonourable. Everything must be surrendered
to the claims of enlightened conscience. There are
limitations to the individual responsibility of an agent,
which cannot be expounded here; but the pure-minded
youth will hasten to free himself from engagements
which involve falsehood, fraud, or provocatives to
sin in others, such as intemperance, and licentiousness,
and desecration of holy time. The higher we go in
mercantile ranks the more we find equivocation and
disingenuous *finesse* to be denounced as short-sighted
and obsolete. Yet among the thousands of city
merchants there will be an admixture of those who
deal by craft, the "wisdom of weakness," and who
exact the like of their dependents. But the disguised
sharper who orders an honest man's son to utter a lie
in his name to customer, creditor, or government should
expect either to be cozened in his turn, or on the spot
to be abandoned and exposed by the indignant youth
whom he would corrupt.

In a class of persons comprising so many men of

honour and men of breeding as is to be found in those
engaged in mercantile pursuits, to say nothing of
morals and Christianity, it is mortifying to find some
who resort to ignoble means of alluring customers.
If a young and uncorrupted rustic falls into such
hands I can only advise him to seek speedy deliverance. The entire affair of flash advertisements, decoys,
runners, and what is known by the slang term *ting-
ing*, belongs to a system which high-minded commerce has long since outrun—the system which led
Cheapside shopmen to cry to passers-by "What d'ye
lack?" which lingers in the market-place where
herb-women twitch your sleeve and laud their
wares; and which may be seen full-blown among
Petticoat Lane Jews, who wrangle and fight for
the privilege of investing some stranger with a half-
price coat.

From this disagreeable topic let us pass to what
some have named THE LESSER MORALS; and among
these, as certainly pre-eminent, the care of HEALTH.
Neglects here come back with vengeance in after-life.
Let us leave out at this place the horrible vices which
poison the blood of youth and send rottenness into
the bones. Smaller errors may destroy health. The
varieties of mercantile life cannot all come under the
same rule. There is a difference between desk work
and street work, between day work and night work,
between long and short hours. In general it is the
sin and shame of mammon-serving employers that
they arrange the times and degree of business with
little reference to the health and improvement of those

whom they employ. Engrave it over your humble
mirror, that temperance, cleanliness, and exercise will
make you hearty and alert. "The three best doctors
are Dr. Diet, Dr. Quiet, and Dr. Merryman." Con-
tinual meddling with the animal machine is not the
way to promote health. Asking whether this will
hurt or that will hurt generally ends in a state in
which everything shall hurt. When Dr. Johnson's
friend Taylor happened to say that he was afraid of
emetics for fear of breaking some small vessels,
"Poh!" said the old Doctor, "If you have so many
things that will break, you had better break your
neck at once, and there's an end on't. You will
break no small vessels." "And then," says Boswell,
"he puffed and blowed with high derision." If a
young fellow is regular in his habits and moderate in
his food, and if he abstains from tobacco and alcohol,
he will probably have cheerfulness and strength.
Many of the neuralgias, dyspepsias, palsies, and
melancholies of later life arise from the cigars and
suppers of boyhood, and their consequences.

Health is promoted by early rising, cleanliness, and
temperance. "Cleanliness is next to godliness," says
the proverb. Scrape the surface with a dull knife and
you will learn why it is not enough to wash for the
public, cleansing only what is visible. These are not
trifles, as the biography of all long-lived men will
demonstrate.

While I am upon these lesser matters I must be
allowed a word or two upon the subject of Dress. The
garb, in some sort, expresses what is within. How

many an employer has instantly rejected an applicant because of a gaudy shirt-pin, a flash waistcoat, and a heavy vulgar chain across his stomach. Sharpers, gamblers, and foreign adventurers carry the most ostentatious jewellery, which is the mark, not of wealth, and not even of fashion, but of vulgarity and upstart pretension. The most elegant dress is just that which no man can remember after you have left the room. Youth need not array itself like age, but there is a modest reserve which commends even the youthful person. Everywhere a young man loses caste with such as know the world by dressing beyond his means. The habit of extravagance in apparel leads to undue expense, and is a particularly bad sign in one whose salary is small, and whose parents are poor. A fop is a fool as truly as a sloven is a savage. On this head I am reminded of what may be called congruity in dress. You shall see a raw young fellow whose extremities do not match any more than Horace's mixed animal. Above, it is winter, below, it is summer; furs and white trowsers; no greatcoat in snows, and pumps in drenching rains. Chief-Justice Hale used to say that he formed a judgment of young men from their knowing how to take care of themselves in dressing suitably to the weather. Attention to one's clothing in trunks and drawers at lodgings belongs also to good husbandry in youth. Let me peep into these repositories unawares, and I will tell you how far my young master is a person of method, and how far he spares trouble to the toilsome needle-woman, whether sister, aunt, or mother, who has the charge of his wardrobe. All these things, especially in one away from home, connect themselves with thrift, advancement, and even inward character.

From dress and ornament the transition is natural to manners and bearing. The same principles govern both. Nothing but the examples of good society can insure genuine polish in a young man; but good sense and good taste influence him to choose and follow one example rather than another. The grand fault of many young men is pertness. To this, it must be confessed, the airy chat of the counter and the warehouse directly tends. Forward, ill-bred boys take this case for elegance, when it is only effrontery. Rules cannot be laid down on a matter so impalpable; but two or three maxims will not be denied. Nothing is well-bred which is presuming or devoid of modesty. Quick, loud accost, and utterance of slang terms, designate the pretender. All this glitter is not gold, but pinchbeck. Good manners are not indeed sheepish, but quiet. Undue eagerness, even with a customer, is ungraceful, and misses the mark. Wherever you see a man of accomplished manners you find one who treats even the humblest person with respect. Indeed, in no one word is genuine politeness so comprehensively summed up as in *Deference*. This is to be practised and acquired in hourly intercourse. For which reason pray avoid the Tom-Dick-and-Harry manner, even with your comrades. Rely upon it, the truest armour against uncivil obtrusion is courtesy to all around you. It is very true, as Cowper, in a poem called " Friendship," says,—

"The man who hails you Tom or Jack,
And proves by thumping on your back
His sense of your great merit,
Is such a friend that one had need
Be very much his friend indeed,
To pardon, or to bear it."

As a class of men, it must in justice be said that merchants are remarkable for ease and propriety of demeanour.

As the manners, and to a certain extent the morals, of every man are dependent on the society which he keeps, this deserves special attention in the young. It ought to be admitted on all hands that young men engaged in merchandise need some associations beyond those which occur in business. If by some chance the youth has access to the house of his principal, it is well; we all know how rare such is the case.

If good companionship is not afforded there will be a resort to that which is seductive. So far are we from abridging this disposition to spend a portion of spare time in agreeable company, that we would enjoin it as a means of improvement. Nowhere is the young man safer than in the houses of his friends. Especially is the company of intelligent and refined women a cordial and a medicine, cheering to the jaded spirits, and preventive of a swarm of vices. The shy and boorish temper which studiously shuns all intercourse is sometimes found allied to moral obliquity. No greater favour can be shown to a youth exiled to city business, than to introduce him to a fireside which he may freely and often approach. The Good Samaritan was not more merciful than he who descends from his status of wealth or dignity to take a poor boy by the hand, and lift him over the awkwardness of the strange threshold. It is, moreover, the facility afforded for enlarging such circles of evening enjoyment which causes us to set a high social value upon church con-nections, which smooth the young man's way to liberal and improving friendships.

Whatever differences exist between kinds of busi-ness, all men need relaxation of soul after the day's work. You may tell them to forego all entertainment, but you talk against nature; the thing is impossible. Nor are those the best men who never seek to be amused. The field for such entertainment is happily spacious; but young men of business are not cared for in the arrangements of society. The thing manages itself in rural districts, but rational recreation must be laboriously sought for in town. And who can ex-pect of the young to make toilsome circuits to gain a safe pleasure, when gaudy indulgence beckons them at every brilliant street corner? After many years of observation I declare my sad conviction, that society has yet to reach a great reform in the matter of inno-cent and healthful recreation. The duty of the moral teacher is not completed when he has exercised his censorship over amusements which he pronounces noxious; it is demanded of him to show some which are benign. The absence of any concerted scheme in our large cities for recreations, scientific, literary, musical, or gymnastic, to which, as to the ancient Palæstra, our careworn youth might resort, is a defect which clamours for supply.

But in the very degree in which we hold that society is wronging its sons by failing to provide, on a large scale and with inviting accompaniments, generous pastime and healthful joy, would we sternly charge the young man to resist the temptation to sinful pleasure. It is one of the first dangers of the novice from country life. The earliest of his city evenings sometimes settle his fate. The half-intoxicated rustic sees fairyland in the common saloons of merriment. Theatrical amusements exercise a powerful fascination. This has been so in all ages. Late hours at places of public amusement conduct to all the rest,—to drinking, gambling, and unholy love. Under the guidance of some new companion—a veteran in vice, a demon in seductive power, ready to turn the bolts of satire against country prejudices and childish superstitions—the flexible youth goes, only half-consenting at first, to have his eyes opened. What can be more abominable than the wish and purpose to debauch the conscience of an innocent boy! I would gladly persuade every such young person to peruse and re-peruse the lessons of the wise man upon a delicate but momentous branch of this subject.*

Can it be necessary to put any intelligent young man upon his guard against those dazzling assemblies, by whatever names disguised, where nocturnal hours are spent in promiscuous dancing? The gauze veil hardly conceals, even from the most unsophisticated, the neighbouring lures of the cup and the courtezan. Young man, in regard to a variety of exhibitions and re-unions which cannot be detailed, ask yourself before

* Prov. vii. 6-27.

you cross the threshold, how you would like to conduct thither a pure and lovely sister.

Let no youthful reader think my caution over-timorous when I earnestly whisper in his ear, MY SON, TAKE CARE OF YOUR EVENINGS. The morality of most young persons in city trade may be judged by the way in which they pass these hours, especially after dark. Happy are those beyond expression who have a home where they can spend these—probably the happiest hours of life—with the mother, the sisters, and the domestic friends; and who have not taken the fearful step of disliking and shunning this shrine of virtuous love. Happy, in the next degree, are those who, though among strangers, have found the path to cultivated and Christian circles, uniting relaxation with progress in knowledge. Happy also, as connected with these, or even in default of these, are such as know the charm of books, of libraries, of scientific lectures, of literary gatherings, and of meetings connected with any of the fine arts. Happy, in no common measure, are the followers of true religion, who learn to employ a portion of their time in assemblies of devotion, or of fraternal converse and philanthropic effort. But amidst all diversities one thing remains fixed. If the evening and night are misspent the youth is hurrying towards downfall. Almost all the corruption of young men is perpetrated by night. Well may you pray to God to cast a sacred shield of guardianship around these hours of exposure!

It is the more necessary for the young man in a strange city to be resolute and decided in this matter, because he has to make head against a strong torrent of circumstances. Those who have mastered this tide and reached success are too often indifferent about the poor fellows who are still struggling. I must say, with much earnestness, the state of society in our cities is not favourable to the improvement of young men. In a great number of instances they may be said to be homeless. Their solitary chambers afford no invitations except to sleep. There is often no cheerful apartment where they can feel themselves to be welcome. The mansions of their employers are, of course, out of the question. But without are bright streets and gay companions, decorated halls, warm in the wintry night, and resonant of music. How irresistible are these temptations to the minds of such as are not forewarned and protected by sound principles of morals and religion; and how many hundreds of youth every year become corrupted by the nocturnal allurements so strongly in contrast with their forlorn lodgings! But great as the temptation is, it must be manfully resisted. The struggle just at this juncture is often for life, nay, for more than life. Here, at this very point, upon this very question how one's evenings shall be spent, the road forks, and bliss or woe are on the right hand or the left. Every unprotected young man should hasten to place himself in connections which may afford motive and means to shun evils so direful. Those, likewise, who come to wealth and influence should use all endeavours to introduce new elements into our social state, so that it may no longer be true that thousands of youth, the hope of coming generations, are in this respect aliens and orphans during the most tempted hours of life.

When we mark the powerful drawing to the night-cellar, the low concert, the ball, the equivocal show, the billiard-room, and the den of infamy, we are led to rate highly every hopeful or even innocent attempt to create counter-attractions. At the risk of all sneers I will maintain that they ought to be multiplied a hundred-fold; as they ought also to have the countenance, patronage, and frequent presence of our established merchants and other men of wealth. Lectures, schools of art, collections of books, of plants, of minerals, of statuary, of painting; societies for composition, recitation, debate, music, varied entertainments; for whom, I pray, should these be furnished, if not for our cherished youth, who are to be the great commercial leaders of a more adventurous age? Let no labour and expense be thought too great when such objects are at stake; and let the warmth of general interest in the movement convince the young persons who are primarily concerned how great are their hazards, and how important the struggle for deliverance.

Such contemplations as these show us the value of early mental discipline. It is cruel to curtail a boy's preliminary schooling without urgent need. The young man should bless God if his parents have secured to him a good education, even in rudiments; and if he be wise he will consider every one of these precious attainments a foundation to be built upon. True it is that the city clerk has few hours for study, but even moments should be husbanded; and it is wonderful how much odd moments may accomplish. Half the moral downfalls of young men in mercantile houses arise from the want of intellectual excitements. In the absence of these, and to flee from the horrors of ennui, they must run out of doors for animating objects. Nothing is more restless than youth; nothing more craving of rapid pleasures. But ignorant young men do not know what elevated and exquisite pleasures are to be derived from the pursuit of knowledge. In this view of the case, we set up a great barrier against vice when we infuse into any opening mind a taste for reading. If considered only as a means of amusement, and as counteracting the seductive objects above mentioned, books may be ranked among the most valuable aids of mercantile discipline. He who is thoroughly awake to the pursuit of knowledge will be unlikely to roam the streets with swaggerers or intoxicate himself at drinking-places.

On this cardinal point of my whole subject let me crave the attention of the young man whose eye may be upon my page. My dear young friend, it is impossible to exaggerate the importance of what I am now advising. It were little to say that by mental culture your power and your happiness would be doubled; say rather you will live in a new world, and be another man. The young merchant is not expected to become an erudite scholar, or a profound philosopher, though such might be named; but there is no one who cannot acquire knowledge enough to be his great profit and unspeakable delight. " Knowledge is Power," said Lord Bacon. " Knowledge is Pleasure," we may add with equal truth. Say not that such pleasure must be earned by long pain. It is untrue. The early obstacles are only for a moment, and the subsequent pursuit of knowledge is so purely pleasurable that I have often paused and sat in amazement at the blindness and folly of those who, with every opportunity and free invitation, never enter on it. " We shall conduct you to a hill-side, laborious indeed at the first ascent; but else so smooth, so green, so full of goodly prospects and melodious sounds, that the harp of Orpheus was not more charming."*

The objections which are now rising in your mind are groundless, and would instantly vanish if your desires were right. You say the acquisition of knowledge is a great work. True; but you are not to do all at once. Step by step men cross continents. Constant dropping wears away the stone. Sands make the mountain; moments make the year. You say you have no time. I wish the over-heated business customs of trade and the cupidity of capitalists allowed you to have more. But let us look this spectre in the face. There is not one man in ten who does not spend some hours in idleness, if not in vice. More may be learned by devoting a few moments daily to reading than is commonly supposed. Five pages may be read in fifteen minutes; at which rate one may peruse twenty-six volumes, of two hundred pages each, in a year. See how much might be saved from sleep, from the street, and from the objectionable amusements of the evening. You say you have none to guide you. The

* Milton.

best scholars and men of science will tell you that by far the most valuable part of their education is that which they have given themselves. Volumes have been filled with the autobiography of self-taught men. Think of Franklin the printer, of Linnæus the shoemaker, of John Hunter the cabinet-maker, of Herschel the musician, of Dollond the weaver, of Burritt the blacksmith, of Hugh Miller the stone-mason, and of Stephenson the engineer. Love learning, and you will be learned. Where there is a will there will be a way.

Begin at once; begin this very day. Take time by the forelock, and remember that the first step is the most difficult. Having begun, resolve to learn something every day. Strike the blow, and avoid the weakness of those who spend half of life in thinking what they shall do next. Always have a volume near you which you may catch up at such odd minutes as are your own. It is incredible, until trial has been made, how much real knowledge may be acquired in these broken fragments of time, which are like the dust of gold and diamonds. Your journey will be made lighter, and even shorter, if you have a companion; and be assured that there is no man of real learning who would not take pleasure in lending a helping hand to a beginner. You will thank me some day for drawing you away from common pleasures to the luxury of books. Lord Brougham speaks well concerning the pleasure of study, and its unlikeness to the low gratifications of sense. "While those hurt the health, debase the understanding, and corrupt the feelings this elevates and refines our nature, teaching us to look upon all earthly objects as insignificant and below our notice, except the pursuit of knowledge and the culti-vation of virtue ; and giving a dignity and importance to the enjoyment of life which the frivolous and grovelling cannot even comprehend." Dugald Stewart, in reference even to those who begin late in life, observes to the same effect,—" In such men, what an accession is gained by their most refined pleasures! What enchantments are added to their most ordinary perceptions! The mind awakening, as if from a trance, to a new existence, becomes habituated to the most interesting aspects of life and of nature ; the intellectual eye is ' purged of its film ;' and things the most familiar and unnoticed disclose charms invisible before." More true than of the pleasures of Vicissitude are the poet's famous lines, when applied to this case of one awakened to the charm of knowledge,—

> " The meanest floweret of the vale,
> The simplest note that swells the gale,
> The common sun, the air, the skies,
> To him are opening Paradise."

This is no place for unrolling the chart of studies. But there are some which seem particularly to invite the notice of one who expects to be a merchant. The command of a correct and easy style is perfectly attain-able, and cannot in our day be left unsought without great loss and poignant mortification. Arithmetic and accounts are so much matters of trade that it seems officious to name them. The history of our own country, besides being delightful to every young man, has a particular bearing on business. Add to this so much of the history of trade, and its progress, legislation, and restrictions, as may conduce to the knowledge of public and international economy.

From what has been said concerning the evening entertainments of city youth, something will at once be inferred concerning the value of associations for social ends and mental gratification. These may be compared to the two fruit-baskets of the Hebrew prophet,—" Figs; the good figs, very good; and the evil, very evil, that cannot be eaten, they are so evil" (Jer. xxiv. 3). What they need is the guidance and protection of superior minds, the wise patronage of society, and the sustaining and corrective pressure of parental interest. Their plans are too momentous to allow of being separated from the best counsels of benevolent and learned men. The clubs which young men get up among themselves are not merely sometimes frivolous and fruitless, which is a lesser evil, but often become the arena of wrangling debates, with quarrelsome results. Society at large, especially that governing part of it which comprises our mercantile weight and wealth, should consult its own interests enough to cast an eye upon the nocturnal dangers of persons in their employ, and to devise means for mental pleasures which are as true and as necessary a part of general education as the school or the college. As the matter now stands, we would exhort the young man who is away from home to attach himself to some group of friends who are at once virtuous, well-bred, and intelligent, for some stated fellowship in improving

exercises. Those who know the world will testify
that it is always dangerous for a young man to have
many evenings in which he has to cast about him for
something to give entertainment. Among the social
pleasures one of the highest places should be given to
Music. Meetings for musical practice, when sternly
guarded against convivial accompaniments and after-
pieces, are among the long-remembered oases in a desert
life. We have dwelt much on this subject of evenings
and nights, with their enjoyments, because we know
how large a place it has in the thoughts of every young
man in his hours of freedom from the place of business.
The world needs a jog at its elbow to awaken its consideration of the alliance between virtuous entertainment and good morals.

And now we approach a part of our subject so
grave and affecting that we might well lay down
the pen, and ask the guidance of Heaven in behalf of
the class whose good we contemplate. It is that of
PRIVATE MORALS. We might rest somewhat on the
business side of the question, if it were not despicable
in comparison. For if you look around you in society
you will observe that the cases are very rare in which
an openly immoral man is a good merchant. Even
minor negligences of an ethical kind, such as frequent
gay parties, undue display in furnishing, upstart zeal
for club-life, and what is known as "fast" living, are
observed to damage a man's credit. But we speak of
higher morals, and refer to a higher principle. "The
fear of the Lord is the beginning of wisdom." Religion

and morals must not be severed; for morality is a part of religion, as religion is the source of morality. In a book on practical ethics, the several duties of mercantile life and of young men in business ought to be catalogued; but within these limits we can only deal with general maxims, exemplifying these by a most sparing selection of particulars.

The chief thing is PRINCIPLE. No empirical rules, no imitation, no regard for outside or for gain, can take the place of inward purity and right. Consider what is meant by a young man of principle. He is not so much one who does or avoids this and that, as one who acts from a heart-spring of perennial conviction as to duty. He is principled by intelligent conscientiousness. He works by rule. He carries within a little chart and compass of right and wrong. He may err in details, but he follows his conscience; and when young comrades suggest this or that form of doubtful indulgence, he resolves, however gaudy the lure and however disgraceful denial may be in their eyes, to refuse point blank, and to hold his ground with courage, until he shall have settled the right and wrong of the matter.

This virtue of courage is a great safeguard of youth, but is sadly wanting in most. Thousands of crimes begin in shame or fear about declining a friend's invitation. The novice dreads above all things to be thought "green." The country boy blushes at the charge of rustic innocence. The good man's son is twitted with his "governor," and is asked whether his mother knows that he is out. Imbecility and cowardice are not proof against the assaults of ridicule, and so become an easy prey. " He goeth after her straightway, as an ox goeth to the slaughter, or as a fool to the correction of the stocks; till a dart strike through his liver; as a bird hasteth to the snare, and knoweth not that it is for his life" (Prov. vii. 22, 23). The only adequate provision against such emergencies is found in perpetual regard for the presence of God, and immovable determination to observe his law.

Without courage, there will be no truth; and without truth, no honour and honesty. Nor will there be any of these without reverence for God. To lie and to swear falsely are parts of ungodliness; both exist extensively among unprincipled mercantile men. Inward truth is the beautiful base of the whole commercial column. Abhorrence of falsehood, in all its even tolerated forms of prevarication, equivocation, and evasion, should be cherished by the commercial novice concerning himself, as it is universally entertained by wise employers in regard to such as apply to them. Whatever fair colours we may put upon them, all the deceits of trade are so many lies, and all the deceivers are liars. Men will draw blood if one gives them the lie, as it is called, who will, nevertheless, daily utter and act the lie at the counter or in the street. The foundation must be laid early, and the trial of a boy often involves something akin to martyrdom. No youth is bound, or even allowed, to lie for his employer or lie for his living, and if the question be, "lie or die," no heroic fellow will doubt which to choose. The same reverence for God will govern every young person of principle in regard to the more solemn sanctions of the oath. However ignorant and loose minds may regard the kissing of a book, in the police courts or elsewhere, as a mere form, every oath is an act of worship, an appeal to the heart-searching God as witness, and an implicit imprecation of his judgment in case of untruth. So nearly allied are integrity of word and of deed, that the common people are not far astray when they say, "He that will lie will steal," which naturally leads us to the next topic.

Honesty, in the common meaning of the term, is the cardinal virtue of trade. Integrity in matters of business—namely, justice between buyer and seller—is clearly the bond of union among all who engage in exchange of value for value. To put the matter on the footing of the adage that "Honesty is the best policy" would be looking much too low. Bright honour in all that regards property is the dictate of enlightened conscience, and is pleasing to God. Principles of honesty are implanted early,—perhaps at an age earlier than the entrance upon the most juvenile business. The community is startled when some great swindler absconds, leaving hundreds of widows and orphans beggared by his monstrous frauds. But the flood which has now burst its banks began to trickle many years ago; and close inspection will perhaps show that the princely villain has long been living in breach of other commandments besides the eighth. There was no moral principle.

So wide a subject cannot be discussed in two pages. We warn, we charge, we beseech the youth who enters a mercantile house to pray that he may not be led into temptation. You feel safe; but so have others—so have all felt. The sight and handling of money works changes in the mind. Where there is chance of appropriating what is another's, he who does not fear God will brave the risk of detection. It is not only perilous but destructive to admit the treacherous thought that the pettiness of the crime removes its guilt. Equally delusive and ruinous is the pretext which commonly veils the beginnings of embezzlement, that what is abstracted shall be replaced. Theft is so odious that the poor creatures who purloin from their employers do so under some fairer name than that of stealing. Yet such it is, whether by detention of funds, false entries in books, deceptive representations as to value, concealment of errors, or connivance at the petty tricks of others.

Ingenuous youth ought to be made acquainted with the fact, which we derive from merchants of the highest respectability, that cases of private dishonesty are much more common than appears by any public statement. In banks, in offices, in shops, the unwary young man is led to appropriate what is not his own. Detection follows; but to prevent exposure he is quietly dismissed — perhaps at some future day to figure in the police reports of a foreign land. It is an established fact, familiar to all observers, that larcenies, and frauds of this nature, connect themselves, in a majority of instances, with more common and venial faults, against which the inexperienced should be warned. For example, the straitened clerk, whose parents are poor and whose salary is scanty, has been silly enough to contract debts which he is unable to pay. There is a propagative power in debt, and he finds himself sinking deeper and deeper; it is one of the great reasons to deter from becoming thus involved. Instead of making a clean breast of it to parent or employer, he abstracts a portion of what is entrusted to his care, under the self-delusion that it is a loan. Or a young fellow is fond of dress and vain of his person. He dresses and decorates far beyond his means; and in an evil hour seeks to supply his necessity from the property under his charge. Or he has been smitten with a passion for the theatre and its kindred entertainments, and thus is led to tamper with the moneys of his employers. More dreadful yet is the habit of early gambling, itself inseparable from dishonesty, and leading to thousands of small frauds at the place of business. These considerations should operate on persons in such posts as a powerful argument for plainness of dress, temperance in food and drink, and rigid frugality in all expenses. No young aspirant for honourable gain can ever acquire too intense a horror of the beginnings of dishonesty.

Dreadful is the case of a young man who finds himself in the clutches of a principal who is dishonest, and who is expected to forward himself by indirect gains. The victim must either abandon the place or, what is infinitely worse, become a rogue. The emulation of salesmen in busy establishments is stimulated too highly when youth are laid under inducements to make false representations, to conceal known defects, to shuffle about quality or prices, and by word or sign to violate the bond of honour. Short-sighted is the policy which leads any to bring up young men on such principles. Yet he must have lived out of the world who knows not that the frequency of such deceptions, among a certain class, is bewailed by honourable merchants as the opprobrium of their calling. It was this view of the perversion of trade which led the celebrated Gouverneur Morris to write thus in his diary in Switzerland : " I think I have observed in this country that the spirit of commerce has operated in the cities a depravation of morals, which nothing can cure but that same spirit carried still further." Conformably to this, we observe the contempt with which such methods are habitually scouted by great and established houses.

We should greatly sin against our conscience if we allowed any false delicacy to withhold us from warning our young readers against another class of immoralities. We mean such as are offences against the seventh commandment; and these as well of thought and imagination as of word and action. What tongue can tell the horrid, loathsome, damning consequences of youthful impurity, whether social or secret! Could our hospitals, with their lazars, or the more secluded pining and mental ruin of self-destroying vice, be spread before the tempted, they would shudder and fear. Words of unchastity; perusal of licentious books, now, alas! very common; inspection of loose pictures, prints, and exhibitions; and converse on topics which should not be named, are working daily havoc among the young. It is melancholy to know that the dangers are greatest in our cities. The principles of the Word of God, deeply fixed in the heart and conscience, furnish the only sure protection. At this period of life temptation will certainly come; let every young man seek the aids of divine grace. For such persons the history of Joseph is a most valuable study; and myriads have been restrained from transgression by remembering and reiterating his words: "How, then, can I do this great wickedness, and sin against God?" (Gen. xxxix. 9.)

Allied to these, as carnal pleasures and provocative of these, are the indulgences which tend to intoxication. There seems to be but one path of safety to the city youth; it is that of entire abstinence. No method is so simple, none so effectual. It is amazing that any young man, so long as a single shipwreck from strong drink meets his view, should hesitate to save himself from the peril. Here, again, the night hours are full of jeopardy. It is madness to allow yourself, even for once, to be led by jolly companions to enter that illuminated house or drink at that bar. Cry, Avaunt, devil! and pass by. Once entered, you will go again and again. Thus, when you shall have acquired the habit of drinking, you will be possessed not by one vice, but by the parent of many vices. Summon before your thoughts the worst and most ghastly drunkards you have ever known, and then consider that there is not one of these demoniacs who was not once as pure and as fearless as yourself. Keep yourself pure. Contaminate not this blessed period of youth by making it the avenue to possible crimes. The course of temperance is one which in no event you can ever regret.

Above all, set a guard upon appetite and cowardice at the moment in which you are tempted by convivial and less cautious associates. And, as you value your prospects for life and your soul's health, never allow yourself to be caught a second time in the room where there is carousing, or in the street group which turns aside into the depositories of liquor. But, as has been already declared, it is beyond our power to stigmatize vices in detail. The great jewel to be prized and watched is the internal desire and purpose of doing right.

So tender is the relation between parent and child, that where it is not religiously observed there can be no soundness of character. If this is gone all is gone. I have alluded to the fact that so many young men in city life have left parents in other places, and I have always felt that it gave increased interest to the class whom I now address. The first impression on leaving home is always sorrowful yearning; but afterwards there comes in many a stage of neglect, if not of indifference. Hence young men should be exhorted to maintain a constant and frequent correspondence, by letter and visits, with the honoured and beloved home. These divinely ordered attachments are among the safeguards of virtue. Think often, young reader, of the anxiety of those parents on your account; yet the greatest of these throes are as yet unknown by you. These solicitudes have increased as you have grown older, and reached their summit when you left the threshold of your infancy. If those venerated guardians of your life are truly religious persons, you need nothing from me to inform you what is their chief wish concerning you. The happiness of their declining years is very much committed to your trust, and is every way a generous motive for you to be temperate, honest, and successful, that thus you may cherish and shelter their old age, as by a contrary course you may bring down their gray hairs with sorrow to the grave.

Little does the giddy youth guess the conflicts of the parent on whom, perhaps, he has but lately drawn for the supplies which he squanders. In his boisterous and inexcusable nights he thinks not, though it be true, that the aged pair are by the home fireside projecting for him some innocent joy which he has long outlived and learned to despise. The son may be deep in drink, in gaming, in loose enjoyment, when that father and that mother are on their knees before God invoking every blessing on his head, and especially his eternal good. There is many a mother caressing her lovely infant who, if she could foresee his course of profligacy, would rather behold him dashed to pieces while yet a child than live to be his own destroyer. May I not use these familiar but affecting considerations as urgent motives why, in this your absence from home, you should carry joy to your parents' hearts? By industry, by frugality, by purity, by religion, realize that prompting which rises within you. " A wise son maketh a glad father; but a foolish son is the heaviness of his mother" (Prov. x. 1). Not only let a regard for filial duty, and a fear of adding to parental woe, arm you against the seductions of vice, but continually act as in the presence of those revered counsellors; remember their precepts, and ask God's aid to requite them for their love.

Thus you perceive I have been almost imperceptibly led to touch on Religion as the only certain protection from the dangers of the city. It might be set before you as not less truly the cause of worldly happiness. While some dream of fortune, the wise youth will trust in his father's God. "Acknowledge the Lord in all thy ways, and he will direct thy paths." Take the affectionate counsel of one who is growing old, and forsake not the morning and the evening devotion, nor the perusal of that Bible, the gift perhaps of a mother's hand. With equal earnestness do I implore you to regard the day of holy rest, and to go regularly to some one stated place of worship. The habit of roving from church to church is common with young men, but is inconsistent with genuine devotion and improvement. You will be a gainer for life by entering closely into the associations of some Christian church. It will be your Sunday home; it will make you the safest friends; it will give you reputation and credit; it will cultivate social and religious habits; and it will bring you early into active philanthropic habits, for which Christian merchants are unsurpassed. If you have erred in this respect, hasten to retrace your steps. Lose no time in securing yourself a place in the house of worship, and an opportunity of teaching or of learning in some religious class. In some hour of illness and peril you may remember what you now read, experiencing the fraternal supports of Christian affection.

True religion is the perfection of the intellectual

and moral being. It is a secret thing, but of most public consequences. From its nature it is suited to every period of life, but peculiarly beautiful in youth. Infinitely removed from all grimace, superstition, bigotry, and show, it is perfectly compatible with every variety of innocent labour and successful enterprise. Its maxims, principles, methods, and promises you will find in the Holy Scriptures. But especially will you behold it in the Lord Jesus Christ, who is the way, the truth, and the life: true religion is the belief of his truth and the following of his example. In those moments especially when in solitary musing you are made to feel the hollowness of earthly things, recognize the gentle drawing to a portion which can satisfy, and learn that Wisdom's ways are ways of pleasantness, and all her paths peace.

I should greatly fail in my purpose if I left on any youthful mind the impression that religion is merely negative. No, no! When I contemplate the power wielded by the mercantile talent, enterprise, and wealth of large cities, and then see the army of youthful recruits who are pressing forward, I glow with new desire that they may attain a manly, earnest, courageous Christianity. Our best hopes for the Church of the future, under God, is in what we descry of promise in young Christians. Consider what kind of religion is demanded by the period about to dawn. Is not manly earnestness in Christ's cause especially required for the times which are coming upon the earth? No one who has at all kept abreast of the times can give a glance into the future without starting up, roused and expectant, at the probabilities of trying times and near emergencies, which will call for stout hearts and strong hands. The combination of omens during a few years naturally leads reflective patriots and Christians to search afresh into the prophetic oracles; and both Providence and the Word teach us to await a period in which a robust Christianity shall have all its nerve brought to the test. This conflict will involve the capital of our extensive commerce and the mighty men of trade. Woe to the young man who goes up to this battle with weak and sickly habit, with slender faith, and with waning love. In exhortation to the whole class, therefore, I would say, BE MEN, in knowledge, in self-denial, in endurance, in effort, in perseverance, in love. Whatever contributes to your real piety will add to your strength. No increase of outward act, no pragmatical hurrying from toil to toil, no forwardness, no bustle, will make you powerful for good: all these may exist in the absence of both purity and benevolence. But devoted attention to the Scriptures, and private prayer, in such hours as even the busy may redeem for this purpose, will do it; the habit of performing common acts as religious duties will do it; communion with a dying Saviour will do it; the "unction from the Holy One" will do it. Let me leave with you my vehement charge that you seek a religion higher, broader, and deeper than we your counsellors have acquired in our tardy age, or than you observe around you in a world maddened by devotion to Mammon.

MEN OF BUSINESS:

THEIR

POSITION, INFLUENCE, AND DUTIES.

———————◆———————

JOHN TODD, D.D.

MEN OF BUSINESS:

THEIR POSITION, INFLUENCE, AND DUTIES.

WE have no doubt that had the arrangements of Providence and the whole order and condition of human society been entirely different from what they actually are, it would have been wise; not because we can *see* how it could be, but because we believe that God could not and would not establish any order which would not be wise. If he had so arranged things that every star had shone with equal brightness; that every mountain had been of equal height; that every tree had been of equal size; that every flower had been of equal brilliancy; that every breeze had been of equal strength; that every human body had been of the same proportion; and that every human mind had been of the same powers and faculties, we have no doubt it would have been thus, because this was the wisest plan: but because we see it is not so; that no two things are alike and in all respects equal; that no two waves of the ocean are of just the same height, no two blasts of wind of the same strength, no two blades of grass precisely alike, and inasmuch as we see through all the works of God endless variety combined with

perfect unity—men of different colours, and forms, and
sizes; of different minds and capacities; some lofty
and some lowly; some strong and some weak; some
giants and some pigmies; some rich and some poor;
some active and full of energy and fire, and some timid
or sluggish, we have no doubt but this arrangement is
the wisest possible. Mutual dependence runs through
all the works of our heavenly Father. The dull, gray
lichen, that clings to the rock and draws its life from
the cold stone, is slowly gnawing that rock into fragments so small that the proud tree of the forest may
take it up for nourishment. The planets hang in the
heavens and roll in their orbits by mutual dependence,
balancing and hanging upon each other. Destroying
one, or changing its position, would change the whole
face of the heavens.

Let it be once settled in the mind that Infinite
Wisdom has seen fit to have mutual dependence among
his creatures, and then we can see why under his
government there should be diversities of gifts—why
there should be different stations and positions in life;
some high and some low; some honoured and some
unknown; some rich and some poor; some to plan
and some to execute; some to be like large lakes to
collect the waters, and some like the pipes to dis-
tribute the waters when collected. The wise and the
unwise, the strong and the weak, the educated and
the neglected, the full and the empty, are all mingled
together, and all mutually dependent on one another.
The care and toil and anxiety of the parent, and the
joyous laugh of childhood, and the fresh smile of

infancy are all parts of the happiness to be found in a family. Take any one out, and you take out a golden link. · Hush one voice in death, and you bring a shadow over the dwelling, which will continue to darken it as long as life remains.

Instead of doing away with these diversities of gifts, and breaking up the arrangements of Divine Providence, the Gospel comes in to regulate and guide them, and make them all work in beautiful harmony. There will always be the necessity for laws and rulers, for the different professions, for rich men and poor men, for teachers and pupils, for men to plan and men to execute, masters and servants; and these distinctions will always exist. Some are fitted, in the providence of God, by natural talents, by capital, one or both, to be employers, and some are fitted to be employed.

In a land where the Gospel has roused up the human mind, educated it universally, and created great industry, there will be great wealth; and this wealth must be kept moving, changing forms, and places, and hands. It must find new channels in which to flow, new markets to supply, and create new demands where no demand exists. In heathen countries, where the intellect sleeps and is uneducated, there is comparatively little wealth. Macaulay testifies that India, in its dark heathenism, is one of the poorest countries in the world. In our own country the Gospel has from the beginning so far laid its hand upon the nation that it has educated it, awakened the intellect, called forth new and important inventions, created a great amount of wealth, and put everything

in motion. The streams are harnessed and made to
draw; the earth is dug open and made to yield fire,
and light, and power for machinery; a greater number
of tons of merchandise is annually moved than by
any other nation; manufactories of everything, and
machinery for changing the form of everything, are
everywhere set up. All this goes to create and call
out men possessing a peculiar kind of talent, a peculiar
natural endowment; and these constitute a distinct
and a very important class. I mean what is commonly
called the BUSINESS MEN of the age. It embraces a
great variety of occupations and employments. I
include in it all who give their time and thoughts to
a particular branch of business, such as bankers, insurance companies, merchants of all descriptions,
capitalists, manufacturers, railroad and canal contrac-
tors, master mechanics, shipmasters, and all who
employ others to manage movable property. Modern
cities are built expressly as business-posts; ancient
cities were built for defence. A modern city is built
on a harbour, so as to be easily accessible to the
ocean; ancient cities were built on the river, away
from the ocean, accessible to fertile lands. Modern
cities pay little attention to the question of defence,
and ask no walls; ancient cities made this the great
question. Hence our modern cities are the gathering-
points where business men congregate, and are the
tunnels through which they pour the creations of
human industry. There are several reasons why we
should consider business men an important class of the
community.

I. *The circulating medium of the world is all in their hands.*

It would be difficult to know how much money—the circulating wealth of the world—is in their hands, or how much changes hands daily. This mighty tide is swayed, ebbing and flowing every moment. They have the power to create a panic, to honour or dishonour a nation every day. They can give their city and country a good name all over the earth, or they can carry bankruptcy over a wide domain. There is no earthly power which is felt so quickly or so widely as the power that moves the circulating medium. Half a dozen men in a country bank, though the bank is but a drop in the bucket compared with the real estate in the place, can often control a whole town; and half a dozen banks in a great city often control the city, because they can control the circulating medium. A single manufacturer can throw a gloom, in an hour, over the dwellings of all his workmen. Ready money is ready power; and the men who have all the money of a nation in their hands must be an important class.

II. *They are important because all the movable wealth is in their hands.*

The ore that comes out of the earth, the coal that follows the ore, the products of all the factories, all the workshops, of all the machinery, of all the agriculture, of all the fisheries, in short, everything that can be raised from the ocean, from the land, everything that can be moved on land or on the water, everything that human ingenuity and skill and toil can produce, is in the hands of these business men. It may not be theirs, but it is passing through their hands. It is for them to manage. They may have all the machinery that human ingenuity can invent, and they may have the best and the largest ships that ever sailed, but they must change the form, and the place, and the value of all the property of the world. There is not a farm in the land, nor an acre of ground, nor a cow, nor a sheep whose value is not affected by these men. Their honesty, capacity, activity, energy, and skill make a nation prosperous or otherwise. The beautiful lands of Italy nourish the wild boar, and he can be hunted within two and a half hours' ride from the gates of Rome, and the sunny skies hang over a starving population, because there is no class of business men there, —they are neither encouraged nor allowed, and the land is running to poverty and desolation.

III. *The business men of a nation have most of the activity of that nation in their hands.*

Most of those who are managing and moving all this great amount of property are men in the morning and vigour of life. Youth cannot do it. Age stoops under the burden, and withdraws. The load is too heavy. Your business men must have great bodily vigour, great strength of constitution, incessant application, and untiring labour. It is noticed that in a time of invasion and war no men make such soldiers as business men. This is not because they have so much to defend—the retired, timid, rich men have the property to defend—but it is because they have the habits of activity and energy that make them powerful anywhere. Your man of business, with his pale forehead and anxious look, has often a wiry frame and a body which can evince great endurance, else it had long since broken down. The load is so heavy that multitudes do break down, and fail in business, because they first failed in body, then in energy, and then in judgment. No class of men work harder, as a class; none strive harder to bear up and carry their burdens manfully than these men; and often the intellect is taxed to an extent of which few dream.

IV. *The business men of a nation must have a vast amount of intelligence, and hence they are an important class.*

We do not pretend that these men—each one—knows much except the particular branch to which he is confined. But let any one go into the office where the patterns for a great machine-shop are drawn out of the brain; let him go through the plottings and calculations necessary to build a railroad or to build one great ship; let him sit down and study the markets thousands of miles off, and calculate whether he can deal with one of each country, and a dozen in all; let him plan what fabrics will be wanted two years hence in a distant land, and how he can collect materials and manufacture those fabrics; let him calculate the chances and prospects of war or peace in this and in that part of the earth; let him study how to improve this machinery, obtain a few more revolutions of a wheel in a minute; how to compete with men who have great capital and skill and facilities; in a word, let the man who thinks that the men of business have not a vast amount of intelligence watch them as they roll the wealth of the earth from one quarter to another, as they change a dreary sand-plain into a great city, as they make the air and the water, the streams, the lakes, the forests, the ocean, the winds, and the very lightnings work in their behalf, and he will see that there is, and must be, a great amount of intelligence in this class of men. I have sometimes felt almost indignant when I have heard the success of men attributed to luck and chance, and the intelligence of this class denied. Their success depends first on God, and then on the intelligence, skill, thought, judgment, activity, and labour which they bestow on their business; and he must be very weak or very jealous who denies a great amount of intelligence to our business men.

It follows that this class of men have, and must have, a prodigious influence upon human society. They make or unmake a nation. The professional men are few in number compared with the men of business. They have in their hands but little property. They move but little. Their influence is of another kind. But upon the men of business hangs the question of plenty or want, activity or stagnation, hope or despair. Men must look to them. Labour looks to them for employment, for direction, and for reward. Poverty looks to them to feed the hungry. Our schools and colleges, and all that pertains to the education of the nation, the elevation of the human mind, must look to them for the pecuniary means. The ministry can furnish teachers for the young, but we have not money, and must come to you for that, to endow our institutions of education. The ministry must call upon you to build our churches, and support us while we labour for the elevation of society and the conversion of the soul to Christ. You have the wealth, and we must call upon you to aid us, and to furnish means, while we explore the earth, circulate the Bible, and show you how you may here and there use your means for the best good of men. There is not a college in this land, nor an institution of learning, which has not been created and endowed, directly or indirectly, by men of business. The clergymen, the lawyers, the physicians, as classes, have little wealth. They are exceptions if they have, and must get it, if they have it, aside from their profession. We labour, co-operate with those who do the business of the earth; but we must come to them to furnish the means and the appliances of usefulness. A village store has been known to have the circulating wealth, and therefore the power to control the political elections of the village for years. Such a store has been known to do more to demoralize a small town than all other things; and having all this power and influence, is there any danger of my overestimating the importance of having our business men understand their position, their influence for good or for evil, upon the great interests of humanity here and hereafter?

It is hardly possible, as it seems to me, to overestimate the responsibility which the providence of

God has laid upon this class. They owe peculiar duties to themselves, to their families, to those employed by them, to society at large, and to God, the Father of all. And,

I. *They ought to be men of the strictest integrity and honesty.*

No young man ought to look forward to a life of business if he is conscious that it is hard for him to be honest in the smallest matters. If he would defraud his sisters or brothers, if he would take more than his share in a division, if he ever conceals what falls in his way without actually stealing it at the time, he ought never to go into business. When property is passing through your hands continually, when it is so easy to overcharge here and there, to clip a little here and there, to use what is in your hands with the intention of repaying it, you ought to be very careful to be honest to a fraction. As to the plea which some men make, that it is impossible to do business and be strictly honest, I must say with great frankness, I do not believe a word of it. I believe it is just as practicable to be honest in using property as it is to use the tongue without being profane. I have known men grow old as merchants and as manufacturers who were, I have no doubt, strictly honest. A single fall of a clergyman dishonours all the profession; and so every dishonest man in business hurts all his compeers. He tempts others to meet him with the same weapons and to fight him with his own sword. He tempts the whole class to do so, and he tempts the community to look upon the whole class with suspicion. Business men have the very best opportunity to be dishonest. They can cheat every day of their lives, and nobody can detect them. We are all in their hands, and they may grind the poor, and do injustice to the ignorant and the unsuspecting, and we have no redress. They can manufacture, or adulterate, or dispose of a bad article for a good one. By silence they can defraud me. How important, then, that in the fear of God they should make it a rule from which they never swerve, that they will be strictly honest in all their dealings!

II. *The man of business ought to be a punctual man.*

No man can succeed in business unless he is strictly punctual: he must be punctual not merely in paying his debts and meeting his engagements on the day they become due, but the habits should run through everything. He must see that the ship sails on the day and at the hour advertised; that the goods are packed, and forwarded, and delivered, not a week later, but at the very time promised. A delay of a day may disappoint passengers in his ship, or it may detain the goods on their way over a whole season. The habit is transmitted to others, and if you are not punctual and prompt, those under you will not long be so. The manufacturer is careful to bring his workers up by the bell; and the merchant ought to insist upon it that his warehouse be opened and closed at just such a time, that everything sold shall be delivered at once, that bills shall be collected and paid promptly, and

that neither he nor his customers shall suffer for the
want of promptitude. The loss of time and property
by delay and slackness is incredible. You are, perhaps,
building a large factory which has been burned down.
You want it covered with slate. You send to the
builders and inquire if you can have so many slates,
and at what time. They reply, yes, you can have
them, and name the day when they shall be forwarded.
You go on and put up your frame, and get all your
carpenters on hand, but no slates come. You write,
but it does not bring them. You send a special mes-
senger all the way to the quarry in another town, and
he finds that a fortnight after the time appointed the
slates are not shipped, or even all out of the quarry!
And so you have the loss, and the disappointment,
and the vexation, and all because the man who made
the promise is not a punctual or a prompt man.
There are ten thousand such cases occurring continually;
and the loss in property, in time, and in character, is
beyond computation. Every man living, who deals
with men, has suffered more or less in this way. You
might as well deal with a tailor who only basted your
coat as with such a man. Every unpunctual man
forfeits his word, disappoints expectation, and brings
reproach on his class. It is most grievous when professed Christians are thus slack. The temptation to it
is very natural. We are weary, and if we can put off
a duty we hope it will be easier to-morrow. It may
demand more of resolution, more of nerve, more of
strength, to be always vigilant, always prompt, always
active and efficient, but you cannot succeed in busi-

ness without all these. Instead of being surprised that so many who undertake business should break down, with the strength, and hope, and courage gone, I am rather surprised that there are not more. I have far more charity for men who fail in business than I used to have before I knew how long and how hard they struggled and staggered under the load, and how they came out of the contest, for which they were never fitted, with shattered health, with loss of self-confidence, with hopes that are crushed, and with the future covered with clouds. And probably these cases are far more frequent than they would be were the books kept thoroughly and examined frequently, and the soundings and offings of the ship constantly recorded. The mistake is a great one for a man to continue in business when he is not its master; when he finds that he lacks qualifications and adaptation to his business, to struggle on, hoping that some brighter day will come, without courage to cut down expenses, or to look truth in the face. A vessel is swamped and wrecked amid the storms of the great ocean, which would have safely crept along the shore and coasted from harbour to harbour. Every one can think of men who are amiable, and who mean well, but who would be wrecked were they to command a ship in a gale, or grapple with all the difficulties of commerce or of business at the time when decision, promptness, and fearless energy alone can avail. The proper medium between timidity and weak caution and rash confidence is the medium which the man of business needs, and parents who are ambitious to have their

sons become men of business can tell at an early
age whether they evince those traits of character so
essential to success.

And here let me say that the man of business has
need of special care in the training of his family. He
is under a heavy pressure as to time, and can hardly
take time to be economical. He can have but little
opportunity to see his own family. He hastens in at
meal-time, anxiously and hastily swallows his food, the
care and vexations of his affairs perhaps clouding his
face while in the house. His words are few and short,
and, it may be, the irritation which is caused by the
unfaithfulness of others is vented upon his family.
His children see that the father has not time to cultivate the social affections, nor time to attend to economy
—that he had rather hand them out five pounds for
a new dress than stop long enough to advise in regard
to one that would not cost half the sum; and hence
they infer that economy is a virtue not held in high
estimation by the father. It naturally turns what
would be love and the refinement of the social affections into the channel of dress. They see the father
handling a great deal of money, and do not realize but
it is all his own; and hence come habits and expenses
into the family which the rich only can meet, while he
is struggling to manage the capital passing through his
hands so as to carry on his business. His family think
him rich when he is poor. They draw upon him
under a mistake, and he meets the drafts because he
is too much hurried to correct the mistake. His
daughters are tempted to want to make up for the

desolations of the home caused by the inability of the
father to cultivate the heart and the affections, by
showy furniture, ostentatious equipage, and extrava-
gant dress. The sons are tempted to feel that while
the father drudges early and late, and keeps his business going, they cannot fail to be rich, and they may waste
time or property, or both. The great temptation
of business men, as it seems to me, is the attempt to
accomplish too much, to do too much, and thus to more
than exhaust their time, their strength, their intellect,
and their affections. They want to get over the point
of danger, to weather the cape of poverty, and sail
into the straits of thrift, too quickly. They cannot
wait for anything that moves slowly. They have not
time to do justice to their children in their training.
Hence it comes to pass, too often, that a business
that has become established and prospered by the great
and life-long efforts of the father, instead of being
carried on by the sons, passes into the hands of the
poor boy who came from the country as a clerk, and
the property which was earned by such untiring efforts
is spent before it was fairly owned, and the sons and
daughters who, a few years ago, seemed to be on the
top of fortune's wheel, are cast down out of sight. It
seems to me that the point of failure is in the fact
that the man tries to accomplish too much business, so
that he must be absent often, be hurrying all over the
earth in a chase that has no termination, and in gathering in only that he may scatter still wider; so that
he unconsciously neglects his family, and unintention-
ally teaches them to despise economy—not because he

despises it, but because he has not time to teach them
economy. Whereas the children of business men
ought to have the best possible training, and then
those noble and shining characters which sometimes
arise from this class of society, would become common,
and, being common, would be great blessings to the
world.

III. *Business men should learn the true use of property.*

There are three uses to which money can be put:
first, to hoard or use it in business for the sake of its
increase; the second is, to spend it upon ourselves or
our families; and the third is, to use it for the good
of our fellow-men. Formerly, when the channels for
business were few, men were tempted to hoard it, to
bury it, or to put it away where it would be safe, and
yet be on the increase. The temptation at this day
is not so much in that line as to gather it fast and
spend it fast. The struggle is to see who will live in
the best style, make the most show, excite the most
envy, attract the most eyes, and be foremost in the
race. Every new house must be costlier and better
than the last built, and every returning season, fashion
must invent something more costly than the season
preceding. Hence the race is more eager and more
costly. And let me say in all sincerity, that I do not
believe there is a custom in this country to be more
reprobated than the lavish expenditure of the present
day. It seems to be in the place of nobility, of
old family pride, and of intellectual and moral worth.

But I think that our business men are beginning to learn the true use of money. They are beginning to understand that he who digs a well, like Jacob, which will gush up with fresh water for ages, has done a good and a great deed; that he who has used his money to found a school where the little feet of children will gather, and the hum of young voices be heard, ages after he is dead, has done a good and a great act; that he who founds a professorship in a college will have an educated and a polished mind there instructing young men generations hence; that he who uses his money to stereotype and publish a good book has opened a well that will send forth the waters of life as long as time shall be; that he who provides an asylum for the blind, the deaf, or the deranged, will be ministering directly to alleviate the woes of humanity in all future time; that he who with his money plants a little church among the heathen, or opens a school there, or who circulates the Bible in a new dialect, is opening a fountain never again to dry up. We must have school-houses and school-books; we must have colleges and seminaries, libraries and apparatus, and all the appliances for educating the human mind; we must have churches and ministers, and all the moral appliances for educating the conscience and the heart. And to whom has God, in his wisdom and providence, committed the wealth of the earth? To whom shall we go, when we want the means of alleviating or preventing the woes of the human family? We can go nowhere else but to the men who own and who are handling the wealth of the

globe. And when these men feel that we call upon
them often, and want large sums, too, let them remember that we go to them because they alone have
the means; that it is easier for them to earn money
than for any other class—indeed, no other class can
earn it. It is therefore unquestionably true that we
must and shall bring the wants of our schools, and
colleges, and asylums, and seminaries, and ask these
men for the means to make these fountains of good to
men. It is also undoubtedly true that we must depend
very much on these men for the means of carrying the
Gospel to the heathen. We own, too, that the support of the ministry must rest very much on them.
They are the financial agents of commerce, of manufactures, of agriculture, of education, of occasional and
systematic charity. The business of the world and the
charities of the world depend on them. They will not
deny that their position is that of trustees for humanity,
nor must they blink the fact that they are deeply
responsible for this trusteeship.

May I not say, also, we can scarcely estimate the
importance of having the business men of the world a
pure, elevated, intelligent class of men; expansive in
their views, honourable in all their transactions, noble
and great-hearted in their charities? It is not the
place for a dishonest man; it is not the place for the
small-minded man; it is not the place for the reckless
man; it is not the place for the narrow-minded man.
Everything about the man of business should be above-
board. In their place, the physicians of a Christian
land are a most valuable, important, and indispensable

class of men. Our comfort, our life often hangs upon their judgment and skill. But they move in a particular circle, and money is not their instrument of usefulness. I cannot speak too highly of the sacrifice and the toil which this profession often makes, not only without reward, but without even the hope of a reward. In their place, the lawyers of a Christian land are not useful merely, but absolutely essential, and a sound, conscientious lawyer is a character not to be admired merely, but a character of great beauty. The profession is an ornament to civilized and Christianized society. They are a moral and intellectual police, and the insurers of justice between man and man. But their sphere is peculiar, and they can do but one thing.

While they have rightly great influence, money is not the power they wield. As law and justice are the foundations of governments, we naturally look to this profession to make the laws of the nation, and mostly to manage the machinery of government. The money power of the world is committed to one class of men. I have sometimes heard it asserted that it is mere accident and chance that one man makes money while his neighbour cannot. But I know better. It is a talent. The Bible calls it a *"power."* "Thou shalt remember the Lord thy God; for it is he that giveth thee *power* to get wealth." A peculiar talent is necessary, just as a peculiar talent is necessary for a profession. The Christian ministry must have a particular talent and a particular call to their position, and the ministry wields a prodigious power, though fewest in number by far of all the professions. Their commission is from Christ, and we estimate its importance by his estimation when he gave gifts to men, and by the good they accomplish. But they have not the money power. They live upon what you choose to give them, are honoured as you choose to esteem them, and they cheerfully live and die for you. Now is it not clear that God in his great wisdom has raised up a class of men scattered all over the earth, to attend to its financial concerns, and to transact the business to be done? They cannot be called a profession, for there is no one branch of knowledge which they profess to know; but they are a class, and they wield the quickest power which men wield, and one far-reaching. They embrace much, very much, of the talent, the strength of mind, the mechanical skill of the world; and they have an amount of energy, and living energy, to be found nowhere else. The news, the intelligence communicated, and the comforts and luxuries of life depend on them. If a scholar invents the telegraph, the business man must carry the wires round the globe; if a scholar writes a book, the man of business must print it, and see that it is circulated all over the land. If a great thought rises up in the mind of the scholar, the business man must put it in material shape, and send it forth for the use of all. He is the universal architect, creating all the material enjoyments which men have. Let him remember that he has this high position, that he may have resting on him great responsibilities. Let him remember that God charges him to beware and forget not the Lord God, in not keeping his commandments, and his judgments, and his statutes,—lest

when he has eaten and is full, and has builded goodly
houses and dwelt therein, and when his herds and his
flocks multiply, and his silver and his gold is multiplied, then his heart be lifted up, and he forget the
Lord his God, and say in his heart, My power and
the might of my hand hath gotten me this wealth.
But let him remember the Lord his God, for it is he
that giveth him power to get wealth (Deut. viii. 11, 18).

But in looking at the responsibilities of business
men in the light of the Gospel—to do good to all men
according to their opportunity—there comes up the
very important question, What duties do they owe to
those whom they employ?   And it must be allowed
that the relation between the employer and the employee is a very important one.   The man who has
the power to plan, and also to execute, is a decided
business man.   But for the most part the departments
are separated.   The man who carries on any business
must have others to carry out his plans.   He must
contrive, others must execute.   The general must plan
the battle, the soldiers must carry his plan into execu-
tion.   It is mind using matter; the brain employing
muscle and sinew.   It was estimated that the mind of
Bonaparte was equal in battle to forty thousand men.
The skill and mind of the manufacturer or the merchant are often worth more than the labour of all
whom he employs.   He must take the responsibility
and do all the planning.   Hence he advertises for
hands, not heads—for manual labour, and not mental.

The imperfection of our state is seen in the fact,
that exact justice is impossible among men, however

we may desire and intend it. You may employ twenty
men to work for you, and when you pay them all an
equal sum, you are sure that some have earned more
than others, and their labour was worth more. But
the risk of their being good or bad workmen you assumed when you hired them.

Now, were the thing *possible*, strict justice would
require something like the following:—We will suppose
you are proposing to erect a factory, which is to employ
say one hundred men. Could it be done, let the
hundred men put in an equal amount of money, of
skill, of labour, and then equally share the profits or
the losses. But the trouble is, when you assemble the
hundred men, it is found that ninety-nine have no
capital to put in. They are poor, and can only put
in their labour. But here is another difficulty: they
are poor, and cannot wait through the year for the
dividends—they must live from day to day. And
another difficulty still: there will be some years when
there is no dividend to be made—when the factory
must run, possibly at a loss, and the ninety and nine
are now in distress. So that it is wholly impracticable
to form such a partnership. The same is true of the
merchant, the shipper, and of all kinds of business.
But among the hundred men assembled, there is found
one who has uncommon energy, a balanced, calculating
head, untiring perseverance, and capital in addition.
He now proposes to build a factory, furnish the capital,
manage the whole concern, run all the risks, pocket all
the gains or losses. The ninety and nine shall be
spared all this; and instead of dividing the loss and

gain with them, he proposes to give them so much wages, pay them weekly or monthly, and make these wages sure. Whether the concern is making or losing they run no risks. It seems plain to me that this is the foundation, or, as we say, the philosophy of the relation of the employer and the employee. It is a state growing out of the unequal condition of things in this world. It brings the two parties together, mutually dependent on each other, and creating reciprocal duties and obligations. It is a state of things under the wise appointment of our heavenly Father. Many schemes have been formed to make the condition of all equal; and there have been societies formed and organizations instituted designed expressly to do away with the relation of master and servant, employer and employee. Vain attempt! The experiments are all failures. Complaints are often loud that the employer is unmerciful; that he makes the poor seamstress sew a whole shirt for a few pence when he ought to pay so many shillings. You forget that it is not the employer who regulates the price, but it is that the number of poor females who crowd into the city is so great, and the demand for employment so urgent, that *they* fix the price. Let three-fourths of these starving women go into the country, where there is food enough and work enough, and the price of making a shirt would soon go up. It would be the same thing to the employer. He had as lief pay a high price as a low one, provided others had to do so. He has only to charge higher for his shirt when sold. It is the number of people that want employment that

fixes the price of labour.   If twenty will work for A
at low wages, rather than not have employment, it is
plain that B cannot afford to pay more; and the
employer is sometimes blamed severely because, as it is
said, he cuts wages down so low, when in fact it is the
number who want employment who regulate the
wages.

In all countries the majority of those who do the
manual labour are poor.   They live on their present
income.   They are often deficient in experience, in
skill, in mental endowments, in self-reliance, in energy,
in capital, and, in a word, they have no business
capacity.   It may not be their fault.   It may be the
want of education and early training.   It may be the
combination of circumstances, which they could not
resist or break through.   It may be plainly the leadings and dealings of Providence that has made them
what they are, as it is his dealings and leadings that
make the employer what he is.   The same wisdom that
gives the different colour and shape and value to the
tree, or to the plants that grow in the field, has caused
this diversity in the capacity and allotments of men.

The great fact should be borne in mind that the
dependence between the employer and the employed
is mutual.   If the one is dependent on the other for
daily bread, for prompt and frequent payments, he is
equally dependent on their industry, their faithfulness,
for the advancement of his plans and his prosperity.
It is very plain, from the bare statement of the relation,
that it is the duty of the employer to *pay* his workmen
frequently and promptly.   In Bible times, before fac-

tories and commerce had become known, and when
labour was mostly confined to agriculture, we are
especially instructed that "the hire of the labourers
who have reaped down your fields, which is of you
kept back by fraud, crieth; and the cries of them
which have reaped are entered into the ears of the
Lord of Sabaoth." A poor man does not stand too good
a chance of getting the best article, even if he has the
money in his hand; and if he has to buy on credit
he must pay dear indeed. It is not the rich who
eat the poorest flour, the poorest meat or fish.
The riches of the wealthy are his castle, and none
dare attack the castle. The poor man has no such
castle. The skill and shrewdness which enable the
rich man to gain his property will prevent his being
cheated in his daily purchases. The poor man may
have no such shrewdness; and if you take away his
power of paying ready-money you have probably
enhanced his expenses equal to taking off fifteen per
cent. of his wages. I am afraid that employers do not
always realize how much sorrow and even misery often
grow out of their neglecting to pay the poor labourer
as soon as his work is done. It is simple justice to do
this, and if you do it at a personal inconvenience it
probably will be far less than that which you make
him feel if you do not. The labourer may have a
family at home who are suffering for food, or for clothing, or for medicine. He may have sickness and sor-
rowing hearts there, whose woes will be increased if
the head of the family cannot bring home his honest
earnings. It may not be this man or that man, but

among fifty workmen probably some one or more will be in this condition. The employer may go to his full home, where want is unknown, and forget all this, but a great injustice is inflicted if he does so.

We are aware that the duties owed to the employees are dependent somewhat upon the business done; that the duties towards clerks and apprentices, day-labourers, operatives in the factory, and sailors on the ocean, are different, and that the variety of position is almost endless; and therefore it is that there is so much need of having the conscience enlightened and awake on this subject. A large class of young men are clerks and apprentices, inferior to the master, it may be, only in age, experience, and capital. They may have, and as a class must have, the elements of strong men in them. They are soon to be the business men of the age; and their treatment and training ought to be such that they may be led into paths of industry, knowledge, virtue, and religion. The difference between training up an honest and a dishonest man, a good character and a bad one, is immense. These young men are taken from their homes and placed under your care, to train them, to form their characters, and to make them men. They are followed by the anxieties, the tears, and the prayers of their parents and friends. To see that they serve you during the hours of business punctually, and to pay them their small stipend, is not enough. These young men are exposed to temptations, to bad associates, to extravagance, and, as a consequence, to dishonesty. They walk over pitfalls continually. How easy to teach

them to be dishonest, slippery, tricky, and untruthful!
"Why did not the lady who has just left the shop take
those goods?" said a merchant to his clerk a few years
ago. "Because, sir, she wanted Middlesex cloths."
"And why did you not show her the next pile, and
call them Middlesex?" "Because, sir, I knew they
were not Middlesex." "Young man! if you are so
particular, and can't bend a little to circumstances, you
will never do for me." "Very well, sir; if I must tell
falsehoods in order to keep my place, I must lose it,
though I know not where to go or what to do." He
took his hat and coat and left; and this took place in
the presence of all the clerks. The rest now knew
the conditions were, that they must lie whenever their
employer could gain a sixpence by it. Is such a man
a safe man to form future merchants? And is he a
solitary exception, or is he the representative of a large
class? That young man, thus summarily dismissed,
is now one of the first merchants in the West, one of
the first men in his region, and one of the most useful
men in all that vicinity. If a man teaches his clerk
or apprentice that he may lie for his convenience, the
young man will soon learn to do it for his own. If
he is trained up to be a deceiver and a sharper he will
be one as long as he lives. Perhaps one of the most
difficult positions as to duty is occupied by the man
who has a large number of young men in his employment. He can shape their character and destiny for
this world and the next. To instruct them how to
handle goods or tools, how to judge of qualities, how to
keep accounts, is not enough. There is a great deal

to be done to keep them from temptation. The places where young men are poisoned and ruined are the tavern, the oyster saloon, the livery stable, the bowling alley, the drinking club, and by the violation of the Sabbath. Any one of these will most assuredly ruin the young man. The expense is such that he must be dishonest and rob his employer, or he must over-charge and rob the customers—sometimes both. Then he associates with those who are adroit teachers in the ways of sin. How to prevent young men from going to these places of temptation is a great question. I have known more than one firm require each young man, on entering their employment, to give a written pledge that he would use no strong drinks, that he would never visit an oyster shop, nor the bowling alley, nor the tavern, nor the livery stable, on the Sabbath, and that he would attend church twice on the Sabbath. These conditions were imperative, and instant dis-mission followed their violation. And after careful observation I can testify that these firms never had any difficulty in obtaining as many young men as they wanted; that these rules were almost uniformly ob-served; but that when a young man violated them, and broke his promise, and was dismissed, he uniformly turned out badly. If there is not moral character enough in a young man to submit to such require-ments cheerfully, there is not enough to build upon and make a valuable character. While I would make such requirements absolute, and hold the young man firmly to his promise, I would do more. I would pay him a premium for excellence. I know of one firm who pay their employees punctually the stipulated wages, and at the end of the year give premiums to those who have cheerfully done their best, from £5 to £10 each; and they tell me the case is very rare in which they do not pay the premium and are gainers by it. The sum of money thus spent is more than saved in making the young men careful, saving, prompt, and vigilant. All men are discouraged by hearing only orders, complaints, and corrections. They want approbation, appreciation of what they do, and reward in some shape or other. Do we not all recall times when an encouraging word or a few remarks of approbation have cheered us and encouraged us to do well in future? The stern commander of a war-ship who never speaks but to find fault is feared and detested; while he who at times expresses approbation, and says that this or that is done just as he likes, will have a thousand opportunities afforded him when he can thus express approbation.

I cannot deny myself the pleasure of mentioning here what I may call a model village. It was a wild spot where three brothers commenced a small mechanical manufactory. It was a small place, and out of the way. From the first they made it a condition with their workmen that they should attend church every Sabbath; that they should lay up a part of their wages; that they should use no strong drinks, and the like. They have now between three and four hundred men in their employment, most of whom have families; for when a workman wished to build himself a house he was aided and encouraged to gain and own it in fee

F

simple. The firm have established a reading-room for their workmen, at an expense of about £80 annually; have built and support a day school at a still larger outlay. The result is that many of their workmen have been with them for years—some for thirty years; they are owners of property; they are intelligent— one of the most appreciative audiences I ever had the honour of addressing; and for a model village I do not know its equal on the face of the earth. We may say that here was a peculiar opportunity to set out right and to keep things right; and so there was; but it was rightly improved; and many a village has been started and grown up in similar circumstances where now the Sabbath is desecrated, where few go to church, where spirit-shops are abounding, where there are poor, dilapidated, and decaying houses, and where the marks of ruin are visible on many a human habitation. If the employers through the land and through the world felt equal responsibility for their employees, and as judiciously set themselves to aid them, the whole face of the world would be changed within thirty years. The forging, the purloining of money, the breaking open of letters, the petty thefts of men while young, and their stupendous frauds when older in years, which now ring and echo all over the earth, would be unknown. No employer has a right to the time and strength of his men without feeling that he owes them the sympathy of benevolence. He owes them advice. They will hearken to him as to no other person living. His experience will be invaluable to those who have no experience on which they can rely. Some of our large merchants who have many clerks are purchasing libraries to be at the service of these, and thus save them from the temptations of being out in the evening. And the benevolent heart will find a thousand ways of winning those whom it employs to the side of sobriety and virtue. You can provide seats in the house of God on the Sabbath, allowing each one to select his own church, of course, and then see that these seats are occupied. You can see that one or more religious as well as political papers come regularly for their use. You can see that each one in your employment has the Word of God —that treasury of instruction which will show every young man wherewith he may cleanse his ways. If you will carefully read over the fourth commandment you will see that those whom you employ are under your own charge, and you have the command of God that you shall see to it that they keep holy the Sabbath day. They stand in the relation of children to you in many respects, and you are to see that they externally honour the Sabbath. The modern exaggerated notions of toleration and the sacred rights of conscience have nothing to do with a duty which God has settled. I do not ask, nor will you, that those whom you employ shall attend worship where you do; but if you will raise up men who are worthy to take your place when you are off the stage—if you will raise the character of even the lowest, and create in him self-respect—you must insist upon it that he shall honour the Sabbath.

When you have men under you whose characters are formed, who have grown into the station they occupy, and can never rise above it, you can do a great deal of good by taking an interest in their concerns, and advising with them and for them. You can give that advice about their procuring a home, about their purchases, about the schooling of their children, about the employment of their children, which will be of very great service to them. It is impossible, of course, for one who has had little or no personal experience in the thing for which I am pleading to be very definite; but all know that the clerks of some houses, and the apprentices of some master mechanics, turn out well and make valuable men, while those from other masters turn out poorly. All know that the dwelling-houses around some factories look bare, filthy, desolate, and repulsive; those of others are neat, clean, inviting, and cheerful. All know that the employees of some establishments spend the Sabbath in fishing and hunting, in roaming and drinking; that those of others are sober, well-dressed, well-regulated families, who go regularly to the house of God; that while some men feel no responsibility about those whom they employ—as if they had done all their duty when they had paid them the sum agreed upon, and had seen that they do their work—there are others who take a kind of benevolent and Christian interest in those whom they employ. The clerks and the apprentices are sometimes invited to the parlour and the table of the employer, and the lady shows that she deserves the title by noticing, encouraging, and honouring those whose interests are committed to her husband. These clerks and apprentices will, in a few years, most likely occupy positions as high as yours; and the children of the man who now works in your factory may, by and by, be among the lawyers and judges of the land. We should make the impression on all, that labour is honourable, and that he who cheerfully plunges into labour, and sustains his part well, is deserving of high respect. All the distinctions in our country are but for a day. Those who are at the head of society to-day may be at the foot in a few years; and those who are low now may in their children be greatly exalted. I am not pleading for equality, but for the rights of humanity, and for something higher than these temporary distinctions—that the welfare of men committed to your care in God's providence is a sacred trust, and one of the ways in which you can do good. The great thing which in this country places a man in the position of influence and at the head of his calling is moral worth and talents. In business it is what we call a business tact, including sound judgment, firm self-reliance, prompt decision, and despatch. These qualities depend partly on bodily organization, education, and mental endowments. They are the gift of God, and these are a trust to be used for him to the benefit of your fellow-men. The great mass of society have not these gifts. Now, if with your energy, and skill, and industry you acquire property and do a large amount of business, and thus call around you a large number of men to aid you, I want to impress it upon you that these men are put under your care, not that you may oppress them, not that you may make them profitable to you and aid to roll up an estate, and thus every day put a greater and a greater difference between you and them; but that you may guide them, assist them, and bless them. You must often bear with them. They are uneducated, perhaps. They do not see why one should be rich and ninety-nine poor, perhaps. They wonder why their income should not be as large as yours, perhaps. You must bear with them. I do rejoice to say that men of capital and men of business are beginning to look at this subject aright. There are many ships in which the sailor is taken up from the crowded forecastle and put in comfortable quarters on deck, where he can have air to breathe. Some ships have been built, and as many poor men allowed to take shares as they cost hundreds of pounds to build and fit them out. Many manufacturers have put up beautiful tenements for their workmen, planted their grounds with trees, and in some instances let off a little garden to each family. Many have established Sabbath schools, and sometimes day schools, for their workmen's children. As to profit and loss, mere pounds, shillings, and pence, I have no doubt that any employer who tries to aid, encourage, guide, and care for the people thus committed to him will, in the long run, be decidedly the gainer. A railroad contractor stated that in building a road in South America he had to hire slaves. When his hands were assembled he went to them, and in a short speech informed them that he had hired them off their masters; that he intended to give them good food and enough of it; and that at every Saturday night he should pay one dollar extra to each man who had been true and faithful, for his own private use. As a result, he said, he never had a corps of men work more cheerfully or do better, and that the hundred dollars which he thus weekly paid out was a most profitable investment.

I would suggest, too, that the employer would do well, when he finds a faithful man, to hold out inducements to him to become permanent. Encourage him to get a home of his own. Show him how he may save a part of his wages, and thus pay for it in time. A changing population must be poor, and continue poor; and the operatives in factories who roll round from place to place must be thriftless, poor, and sunken in hope and courage.

Let but the heart of the employer go out in benevolence, and feel the responsibility, and there will be a thousand ways discovered by which he can do good to those who toil for him. When a man places his child in a school he feels that he has committed that child to the teacher, and that he is to do more than to hear the recitations and see that the hours of study are duly observed,—he is to have the training of the whole character of that child. So when a parent commits his son to you, to educate him as a merchant or a mechanic, it is the school to which he sends him, and you are accountable for the whole moral training of the youth. It is a different training from the college, but it is training—a school, and you are the teacher. Will it do, then, to say that if you see that he works during working hours, and is instructed how to work, that is all you are accountable for, and you have no responsibility as to where he spends the Sabbath or his evenings, as to what company he keeps, and what influences are shaping his destiny? How bitterly through life, and perhaps to eternity, many have mourned their want of care in their early youth!

I do not feel that the sin of the employer in this country is that you do not pay your workmen good wages as a general thing, nor that you neglect to pay them punctually; but the great defect is want of sympathy, want of kindness. The proud heart rebels at the decree of God which places it in an inferior position. It chafes under poverty. It magnifies its trials and forgets its mercies. It envies what is above it, and wants to quarrel with the man who furnishes employment. It complains much and often, and wants to complain more than it does. Nothing but kindness and sympathy can cause it to feel contented without the grace of God in the heart. I shall be told, perhaps, that the trials of the employed are imaginary, and that the youth who is turning morose, and feels that he shall never forget his present hard lot, has no reason for all this. Very likely it is so. But if you can, by kindness and sympathy, prevent his becoming soured in temper and spoiled for life—prevent his laying up this and that to think over in future days—it is better far to show that kindness and sympathy, and turn the waters into channels that will be green and fertile through future years. The great amount of suffering among the poor in this country, some would say, is imaginary. I am speaking of those who labour.

In other countries the child that is born in a low condition is expected to continue there. The child of a
servant is a servant, of course. The family of the
operative are operatives, of course. They have no
trouble because they are low, or because they see
means of rising higher. They do not expect it. It is
widely different here. Not a young man here undertakes to learn any business who does not know that
he *may* be at the head of that business in a few years.
Not a boy works in a factory who does not know that
perhaps the owner of all this great establishment was
once as poor as himself; and thus he has not merely
the natural irritation induced by poverty and a
depressed condition, but he has also the impatience
and the irritation arising from the fact that he wants
to rise in his condition, and cannot wait ere he begins
to rise. He forgets that every degree of skill acquired,
every new insight into the business, every exhibition
of promptness and efficiency, is laying the foundation
of what will hereafter make him what he wants to be.

There are trials, temptations, and dangers connected
with every situation in life; and perhaps there are few
in which they are greater than among business men.
They have the means of self-indulgence. There is not
a gratification known to the depraved appetite of man
which money will not procure. They have it in their
power to oppress all other classes in the community,
and especially to be hard and oppressive upon those
who work for them. Laban could change the wages
of Jacob as often as he chose. They have it in their
power to grind the poor, when once the poor are their

debtors. And I need not say that any power which depraved men have is liable to abuse. There is therefore the need of special care, watchfulness, and circumspection, lest you give way to this temptation. I have personally known things—treatment of the labourer as to his pay, as the charges for articles sold him—such as would make the ears tingle. I know, too, that there are trials inseparable from business which are constant, and which are very great.

Life is made up of trials and duties. Every class must expect these; and if your position is more exalted than the average of your race, your duties must correspond. And a beautiful arrangement it is, that our heavenly Father should have waters gathered here and there in great lakes from which a thousand thirsty acres can draw. He disperses and spreads the waters over the whole region by means of these reservoirs. And so he places the business men along through the land, that they may collect, and move, and change the wealth of the world, and thus give employment, and food, and living to the multitudes whom they call in to help them. And thus is a mutual dependence created between men of different capacities and gifts, attainments and powers. The active and the vigorous are delegated to sustain the weak and the imbecile. The quick, powerful mind to look out for the mind that is slow and inefficient. These should be the protectors of those who need protection. These have a conscious superiority, which they wish neither to deny nor to conceal. Is that superiority to be an engine of good or of evil? Will you make it a blessing or a curse to those who come to you to exchange their toil for their bread, who sell their own sinews that they may live?

God is no respecter of persons, and that same wisdom that saw it best to make different orders and conditions of society foresaw that there would always be this relation—the employer and the employed; the mind that plans and the hands that execute. And how careful has he been in his laws, and even in the unrepealable commandments, to make provision for those who serve, so that they shall be a part of his family. It is wise for the master, for his interests will be promoted in proportion as he sympathizes with and takes an interest in those who labour for him. It is wise for the employed, for they can use an experience and a sagacity superior to their own. I have been asked, I know not how many times, how to make the interests of the employer and the employed one and the same. With our selfish hearts it cannot be done; but we can approximate towards it; and I believe the first step must be taken by the employer, and that those who serve him will, as a general thing, be faithful very much in proportion as he is seen to care for them. It is not by giving higher wages than others do that you can do it. You cannot buy an exemption from the binding force of the fourth commandment with money; but it is by aiding assistants to spend their wages wisely, by taking an interest in all that pertains to their families, by feeling responsible for their moral culture. But the master who seldom or never speaks to his employees, who never enters their dwellings, who has no care how they spend the Sabbath, what becomes of their souls, is, as it seems to me, in the light of the Gospel, not doing his duty. He is not doing as he would be done by. They are *your* servants, and if they are so many that you cannot receive them under your own roof, it will not take from you the responsibility. The world is not wretched because we are not all on equality, and some have more mind, energy, and property than others, but it is wretched because we do not our duty to one another. The friction of the machine is so great, not because some wheels are large and some are small, but because they do not move in harmony, each doing its share. Children of one common Father, fed by one and the same hand, our stations appointed by one and the same wisdom, involved in the same fall and ruin, redeemed by the same Saviour, to meet at the same grave-yard, to be judged before the same throne, are we not brethren now?

Oh! I am afraid that in the great day of trial it will go hard, not with the master and owner of the neglected and abused slave merely, but with many who have taken high airs upon themselves because they were not owners of slaves, but who have had men and women in their service for whose welfare they have taken no more interest than if they were slaves! No other man has so much influence with his men as the employer. No other man is looked up to as he is by them. They are his dependents, and he holds their happiness very much in his hand. They are committed to him by the providence of God. He can raise up jewels for the crown of Christ from among their number. He has constant and rich opportunities to do them good which no other man can have. What a pattern ought he to be! What a model!

I am pleading the cause of the great mass of the human family; of all who preach the Gospel, your servants for Christ's sake; of all who labour on the land, and plough your fields, and reap down your harvests; of all who stand or work in your stores, at the forge or at the bench in your shops, who sit at your looms or watch your spindles in the factory; of all who hazard their lives to exchange your property in distant countries; of all who serve and aid in carrying out the plans of the man of business. I am pleading the cause of all who are beneath you in position, and means, and influence; and I charge you that you *are* your brother's keeper. Not his blood merely will cry to God from the ground, but the groans of oppression, the sighs of neglect, the mistakes of his ignorance, the silent agonies of the heart that beats without sympathy—these all cry to God, and their cry comes up into the ears of the God of Sabaoth, and he comes and charges you, " Masters, give unto your servants that which is just and equal; knowing that ye also have a Master in heaven."

MEN OF BUSINESS:

THEIR

PERPLEXITIES AND TEMPTATIONS.

STEPHEN H. TYNG, D.D.

MEN OF BUSINESS:

THEIR PERPLEXITIES AND TEMPTATIONS.

No view of the present life of man can ever be satis-
factory which separates it from the responsibilities
and results of a life to come. We must regard it as
an arrangement of means to an end; as an inferior
state of being which has been appointed as an education for some higher condition that lies beyond; as a
temporary passage of warfare, a contest with foes and
difficulties in the way, encouraged by the hope of
victory, and of the results of victory at the close. It
is to be considered, not as a voluntary, but as a necessary state of being—a dispensation, a pre-arrangement
for man, in the continuance and ordering of which he
is altogether passive; in which his Divine Creator has
fixed the bounds of his habitation, and holds him in its
endurance and accomplishment, according to his own
will.

The acknowledgment and remembrance of this divine
providence and control we must never exclude. By
its foresight and direction every particular scene and
element of this preparatory discipline is arranged and
overruled to the minutest extent of application. And

every work and every secret thing, whether it be good or evil, is to be brought before the divine judgment at the close of life.

The question of personal relation to this scheme of trial, of actual endurance of its appointed operation, or of individual responsibility for its results, is not submitted to the choice of man. We are here to carry out the plan of personal education which God has devised for us, and to finish with a fidelity which is voluntary, and for which He has promised an ample recompense, the successive parts of the obligation which He has imposed. We are here a spectacle to angels and to men. We bear a commission, and are intrusted with a stewardship, in which the great object for us is that we be found faithful. Here our warfare is to be accomplished; here our abiding character is to be formed; here motives and principles of action are to be adopted, regulated, and settled. Here the line of our unending moral being is to be laid out, and our spiritual nature to be prepared for the exercise of the powers and privileges of its maturity.

This is the divine appointment. And however inconvenient or pressing may be the constituent elements of this scheme of education and trial in any particular case, man cannot refuse or escape them. What can he gain by rebelling against that Being " in whose hand his breath is, and whose are all his ways ?" He is to finish as an hireling his day. His duty and his privilege combine to urge him to complete his appointed work with assiduity and cheerfulness, faithful to his trust and conscious of the gains and advantages of his fidelity. His perplexities and temptations are part of the great plan of instruction and guidance for him in the path of duty. And his happiness and his success in all the great ends and attainments or life will depend upon his holding fast this commanding thought of the divine authority, and his own resulting responsibility, in its serious practical influence upon his whole career.

This theory of human life is of universal application. In the general facts of their trial and contest, whatever may be the variety of their circumstances, all men are equally engaged. Order, employment, and industry are the unchangeable requisitions of the great Ruler of them all. In whatever particular scene or relation of this immense area of human duty any individual man may have been placed, he has no time or energies to waste in barren contemplation, or complaints of the comparative difference and inequality observed among them. His simple province is to take heed to the ministry which he has personally received, and to fufil that, remembering that the rule for all is, " He that is faithful in that which is least, is faithful also in much ; and he that is unjust in the least, is unjust also in much." The comparative importance of particular lines of duty or stations of trust he can never adequately estimate. The smallest pin, or the most unnoticed wheel in a great machine, may possibly be the very one on the tenacity or regularity of which, in its assigned position, the harmony and success of the whole depend.

The world in which we dwell is no place for idlers.

Its occupations and toils are accumulated and pressing on each of its inhabitants. Every individual has a distinct duty to perform, a separate work to fulfil, which he alone can accomplish. It is the order of providence as really as it is the precept of revelation, which requires every man to be " not slothful in business; fervent in spirit; serving the Lord." Every agency is in motion. Every living being here is active and engaged. In proportion to the advantages of civilization surrounding are the demands for individual industry and effort. Exaltation in condition is habitually but an increase of toil. Striving, struggling, inventing, contriving, executing, are the inseparable characteristics of the present condition of man. The most self-indulgent in intention is often the hardest worked in fact. A life of purposed gratification is habitually a life of experienced disappointment and sorrow. And the happiest and the most peaceful man is he who, in faithful contentment, the most thoroughly fills up the measure of his work, and occupies most completely the whole circumference of his relations.

The scale of human occupation is immensely extended and varied. It presents a series of innumerable gradations. But the lowest is not less busy in the order of his place than the highest; and the highest is no more free from the obligation of necessary toil than the lowest. The necessity for habitual, constant labour is the universal rule, and there are no exceptions. We are far from speaking of this fact as an evil: indeed, we may consider it one of the kindest arrangements of the Creator's wisdom. To earn his bread with the sweat of his brow, while it has been the result, is also to a great extent the restraint and the remedy of the sin and folly of man. It is not to be regarded as an infirmity, but as an advantage in his condition. In the sinfulness of human nature the obligation to toil is the security of excellence. The burden of labour is the strength of virtue. Man finds himself equally guarded from moral evil, and excited and prepared for moral improvement and gain, by the inevitable law of his being, that every valuable harvest which he may reap must be the fruit of industry alone, and that nothing but thorns and thistles can be the product of his idleness and neglect.

Every man therefore becomes, in the necessity of his condition, a man of business, engaged in the affairs of this life. His enterprises and investments may endlessly vary in their fields, their substance, and their extent. But be they more or less, grander or more limited in their scale, the great law which governs the whole cannot be changed. It is the order of man's present being, the necessity of his nature and condition, to strive and toil in his appointed lot from the beginning to the ending of his days, and he cannot avoid it. His warfare has been laid out before him, and he must accomplish it: his duty and his destiny are in the labours and contests of this necessary condition; and in vain, under any pressure of weariness or rising of rebellion beneath his load, does he endeavour to be free.

The remembrance of this only just theory of human

life is of incalculable importance. It is not a final growth; it is not an end or object in itself. It is in every step a progress towards another and a future scene of experience and display. It is a contest for a peace and a connected inheritance which are yet to be revealed. It is a training, in a patient continuance in well-doing, for glory, honour, and immortality. It is a temporary service of a high and heavenly Master in duties which he has himself prescribed, and the recompense for which is to be awarded in another and far more exalted state than this. It is a probation, a test and trial state, in which great principles are to be the subjects of experiment even in the narrowest condition, and constant and accurate records are to be made of the experiments as they proceed, and the full and final results of them are hereafter to be declared. " Like a refiner and purifier of silver" does the great Judge and controller of all sit, watching with infallible precision the operation which He has instituted, and bringing out with no mixture of error or alloy, the result which he has designed.

This is equally true of every condition of human life. The differences of human conditions, when compared with that relation to God and to eternity which is common to them all, are extremely trifling and unimportant. The fixed habit of the mind of setting the Lord always before it, of doing all things as in his sight, of remembering the account which is to be given to him of each hour and of each work of every passing day, and of maintaining a conscience void of offence towards Him in every relation in which He has placed us, exalts the lowest earthly employment into a heavenly calling, and makes the most extended scene of earthly interest seem in itself a very little thing. "Perfect peace" is the characteristic and enjoyment of the mind that is fixed on God. Happiness for man is invariably the shadow of duty. To make the attainment of personal happiness the object in life is but pursuing the shadow. We lose the object for which we strive, and waste our time and strength in vain. True enjoyment is only to be found in the faithful discharge of our individual responsibility. While we strive and labour earnestly and assiduously in our appointed work, our happiness, without an effort of our own to secure it, becomes the actual and habitual attendant, and our daily advancing experience displays to us the fact, that to use the world, and to dwell in the affairs of the world, merely as the scene of our appointed duty before God, whose favour and loving-kindness are made our life, is the sure and only method of really freeing life from its perplexities, and of enlarging and multiplying the circle and the number of its joys.

And here is the first opening perplexity of the man of business. He forgets this true theory of life. He loses the substance in his vain pursuit of the shadow. The worldly mind presses into the business of the world as the great end and purpose of its being. The wealth, and power, and honour of human life, the varied attainments of personal influence and gain in earthly things, are sought with an earnestness and perseverance entirely disproportionate to their worth, and completely destructive to the higher nature and hopes of man. The fountain of living waters is exchanged in a deliberate pursuit for "broken cisterns that can hold no water."

Man is resolved to be rich; and in the very formation of this purpose, and in the consequent efforts to accomplish it, though he may intentionally involve himself in no actual fraud or crime, in human estimation, he falls into temptation and snares which habitually drown him in destruction and perdition. His whole life is a scheme of insatiable idolatry. The present world itself becomes his object, and the remembrance and desire for God, together with the recognition of his responsibility to God, are banished from his mind. He has set up an idol in his heart, and has instituted a worship before it of whole burnt-offerings and sacrifices, the claims of which can never be satisfied. His whole scheme of world-worship, too, involves a constant sense of degradation and self-reproach, an habitual repetition of conscious violation of duty, and an unyielding fear of final loss and ruin. He has made his whole life a perplexity in the very plan on which he has arranged its occupations and objects. Already has he pierced himself through with many sorrows in the very scheme on which he has framed the purpose of his toil. But who shall pursue such an end as this as the object of life, and remain innocent of great transgressions? This earnest desire and determination for mere gain will involve the inevitable consequence of successive acts of fraud. They may be secret, they may be without responsibility to

man, but they are not the less real, and conscious, and
ruinous to the soul. There is a constant robbery from
God of that reverence to which his authority is entitled, and of the gratitude and remembrance which
his bounties demand. There is an increasing defrauding of the soul of its native desire and privilege of
enlargement for higher and better scenes and occupations by this oppressive encasing of all its energies in
the miserable routine of low, selfish, local, and temporary designs. There is a progressive denial of all
the finer and nobler affections of the heart in the
refusal of liberal kindness to the needy, and in the
artificial stimulating of the spirit of selfishness, which,
like riveting an iron armour on the youthful body,
violently repressing its natural growth, not only robs
it of all its beauty and strength, but adds also the
keenest misery to its inevitable deformity. There is a
solemn and fearful sacrifice of future hope, and resulting glory, and a kingdom which cannot be removed,
for the mere gratification of an earthly appetite and a
low sensual passion. Who can think or speak of this
whole course and scheme of being without a solemn
perception of the dishonour and guilt which are involved in the very adoption of the theory on which it
is framed? And how can the man who starts in his
career with a principle so delusive and false, and so
necessarily disappointing and destructive, wonder at
any perplexities in which he shall be involved, or at
any bitterness of despair in which they may result at
last? He has doomed himself to wretchedness as the
very characteristic of his life, and he must lie down at

last in the bitterest, but most unavailing sorrow, when his whole weary career has been completed, and his mad experiment has been thoroughly tried.

We quarrel not with the ardour and earnestness of an active life. The business of this world is to be pursued, and that with industry and fidelity. But it must be pursued as a line of duty and as a course of obligation, with a constant remembrance of its responsibility and results, and of the divine authority which is to control it, or it will become a scheme of unfailing wretchedness to the man who engages in it. A constant remembrance of God in his commandments and his claims must be the chosen and cherished attendant of the man who would enter safely and happily into the active business of the world. He must be able to say, "I have set the Lord always before me," as much in the affairs of his office, or counting-house, or shop, as in the direct offerings of his professed religious worship. If he be earnest and upright in his motives and plans on this high and ennobling scheme, he will enjoy in the highest degree the prosperity which may crown his efforts, and he will be peaceful and grateful still, though outward losses and disappointments should prove to be his designated trial. Such a man may say of his acquired wealth, like Sir Matthew Hale: "It has been honestly gotten, and it will wear well." And however low his outward condition may possibly become, there will still be a charm and a relish in his dinner of herbs which riches obtained wrongly can never supply. This just theory and remembrance of life will furnish him with constant light, tranquillity,

and peace.   And he will find, as Lord Bacon has
described it, "no less than a heaven upon earth, in a
mind which rests in Providence, moves in charity, and
turns upon the poles of truth."

But here, habitually, the first perplexity of the man
of business occurs.   He rushes into the world as if it
were in itself the appointed end of his being.   He
plunges into the midst of bustling contests for gain
without hesitation and without alarm; he makes a
complete overturn of the whole divine and the only
operative arrangement of his mind.   Everything within himself, and in his relations to outward things
becomes disordered.   He chases after a shadow which
he never grasps.   He exalts into the place of his
treasures, objects over which the wind passeth, and
they are gone.   He dooms himself to be the victim
and the prey of successive disappointments and of
final despair; he sacrifices his calmness of conscience,
his peacefulness of spirit, his sense of dignity, his
freedom of usefulness and intelligent thought, his
future and higher hopes and aims, in making himself
a mere drudge—a slave, to bear an inevitable burden,
and to groan at last in the perception that he has
gained nothing by its endurance.   What a compli-
cation of sorrows hang upon this one error of man!
Covetousness is idolatry, and this idolatry is the certain
parent of wretchedness and despair.

But against this whole train of sorrows the principles and precepts of the Bible furnish a complete
antidote and preventive.   What better scheme for a
prosperous and happy life can be laid out than that

which is so beautifully described by the apostle in his letter to the Philippian Christians? (Phil. vi. 4.) "Rejoice in the Lord alway. . . . Let your moderation be known unto all men. The Lord is at hand. Be careful for nothing; but in everything by prayer and supplication, with thanksgiving, let your requests be made known unto God. And the peace of God, which passeth all understanding, shall keep your hearts and minds through Christ Jesus." Here is a life of business, which is also a life of usefulness, happiness, and rest; every act of which is exalted into worship, and every gain of which is made an imperishable treasure, enduring in the heavens. In the settlement of this one grand principle and question, What is to be the theory and plan and object of your life? we may predicate the whole issue of prosperity, happiness, and final gain, or of turbulence, disappointment, discontent, and unalleviated misery as its result.

This one fundamental principle will constitute the real distinction between the Christian in the business of the world, who is striving to do everything as unto the Lord, and the mere worldling, whose only desired portion is in the riches of the earth, and to whom self is the only god. Both may meet with the same circumstances of difficulty. Both in their passage through an active, anxious life may graze on the same shoals, or be whirled around the same rocks and rapids. But the one has a guiding principle which will lead to certain security in the issue, and the other has adopted a purpose which, however it may give room for an apparently freer course on the way, can lead to no final result but fearful and irreparable loss.

Our present object is with the former, and not with the latter of these two. The idolator of the world we must leave. He has entangled himself in his first step, and every subsequent step is but a further plunge into difficulty and ruin. His only course of safety is in a complete retracing of his plan of life, and seeking by the Divine Spirit to have all things within him made new. The conscientious servant of God in the world, the real soldier of Christ in the affairs of this life, may be called to contend with many perplexities and temptations, but he will not be permanently entangled or disheartened, still less destroyed by them. "Who is he that will harm you, if ye be followers of that which is good?" is the demand of conscious security and success even in the darkest hours of a Christian's warfare. It is for him that we here write. It is for him that we are disposed to consider more particularly and practically the common sources and shapes of perplexity and temptation to which the man of business, in all the departments of human life, is likely to be exposed.

The conscientious man, who is resolved to regulate his whole conduct by the rule of God's Word, in every department of the business of life is exposed to very similar temptations. So far as the mere attainment of worldly gain is concerned he has a twofold object. He seeks the adequate support of himself, and perhaps of a family dependent upon his efforts; and beyond this, the fair and moderate accumulation of means for future independence. Each part of this twofold object may be justly considered, not only as a personal right, but also as a relative duty. Man may toil for them both with a clear conscience and a tranquil sense of his fulfilment of individual obligation, while he does it all in the fear of God, with an obedient purpose to honour him, and with a grateful remembrance of his goodness, "who giveth him all things richly to enjoy." But he will never pursue his path of labour and gain without perplexities, which will awaken constant anxious concern, often exceedingly harass his mind, and sometimes almost disgust him completely with the whole business of life. Often nothing but the stern demands of manifest necessity will be sufficient to control the power of these rising embarrassments in his condition. And he is ready to feel that were he alone, and obliged only to provide for himself, he would rather flee to the wilderness, and live away from all the busy haunts of men, than endure the anxious toil and trial which he is compelled to bear. This is all a part of the divine scheme of his education for something better. And it is by the means of this very process of rising early, and taking little rest, and eating the bread of carefulness, that God prepares his beloved for the rest which he has provided for them.

He must sometimes begin his life of toil with exceedingly limited means for trade or professional skill. He has little, perhaps no capital of his own, on the basis of which he may traffic, or with the provisions of which he may labour. He starts in his course under a pressure of want which, if it sharpens the wits for calculation and contest, also tends to blunt the conscience, and to persuade him to excuse and palliate many a conscious wrong. "Lest I be poor, and steal," was Agur's reason for his prayer against poverty. And its application remains for ever. But poverty is a relative word. Its adaptation to man's condition is not actual and abstract, but contingent and proportional. The young man in business without adequate capital may not be actually destitute of food and personal comforts; but he is without the means of carrying on the trade in which he has engaged with encouraging or compensating success. To this extent he is poor, and must live by his wits. He must make up in skill and sharpness of calculation, and in toil and persevering industry, what he wants in means. And here is often found a very severe pressure of perplexity and temptation. A thousand anxious thoughts arise, and schemes and visions of possible gain, or of triumph over the adversities of his condition, occupy and excite his waking and sleeping meditations. Bishop Hall says it is easy to drive a long team on a large common; but to turn it safely through the narrow lanes, and to guide it round the sharp corners of a city, requires great skill and care in the driver. Doubtless such an experience vastly promotes the individual skill, and when rightly guarded and governed becomes the mother, however severe, of valuable traits of excellence and usefulness, and of a prosperity in after-life which is more than a recompense for all the process of the education. But many a young man in the fairest openings of trade, under the pressure of anxiety in long-continued con-

templation, from this one source, is driven either to
sink beneath the load of despondency or to hazard in
unwarranted and excessive loans the integrity of his
character, the peace of his conscience, and the future
prosperity of his life. It is a contest in which tried
strength and virtue grows with permanent confidence,
but under which feebleness of principle or fickleness
of purpose is sure to fail. In every class of business
the princes of the trade are the men who began with
nothing, and who look around on all the attainments
of their age with the honest gratulation that, under
the divine blessing, they have been dependent for
their success and prosperity only upon their own
integrity, fidelity, and skill. And we cannot regard
the narrow circumstances of the commencement of
active life as a reason for regret, or a cause for sorrow,
for we believe there is no other process less painful or
harassing which will so surely stir up the gift which
may be in a man, and bring out for circulation and
use the veins of gold which may lie imbedded in his
hidden mines. If he be faithful, honest, honourable,
Christian, his early straitness of condition will be an
everlasting blessing. It is a soil that will yield to
appropriate cultivation the richest and the most lasting
fruit. But it will involve care, thought, labour, purpose, and unshrinking virtue, to prevent its becoming
not merely a perplexity in occupation, but a poison to
the soul.

The want of capital is a difficulty which circumstances and periods of earthly business often very much
increase. There was a time in our history, and perhaps

there are still places in our country, in which a very
small capital might be made to appear a very adequate
start in life.   Habits of living were plain and simple.
The expenses of conducting business were moderate
and comparatively small.   But with the rising prosperity of a country these characteristics change.   No
longer can a young merchant, or even a mechanic, live
respectably, as he thinks, in the simplicity of his
father's style.   Dr. Franklin says, "The eyes that ruin
us are other people's."   There is everywhere now an
advanced scheme of domestic residence and furniture
and dress, which seems imperative in its demands.
There is an immense enhancement of all the costs of
trade in every department of its operations.   The
young man cannot launch his new-built barque upon
the sea of enterprise at less than fourfold, perhaps ten-
fold, the cost of outfit and inventory with which his
father sailed.   This is a difficulty apparently not to be
avoided.   If he shrink from places and opportunities
of trade for their excessive cost, he retires also, as he
thinks, from all the possible gains and advantage which
they hold out to view, and loses the very prize for
which he would contend, from a fear of hazard, which
he is tempted to despise as a want of enterprise.   This
whole contingency of profit often turns upon a very
sharp line.   It may be that the question of moving
around the corner of a street may involve half the expense of his scheme of business, and yet hazard the
whole of its profit.   And he must encounter all this
anxious calculation and contrivance in the very commencement of his plans of work for life.   His diffi-

culties are great; the perplexity of his appointed path is most harassing; and too often is he tempted, either by a sacrifice of principle, to make haste to be rich, and thus, by assuming obligations which he can never discharge, practically to "steal," or to sink in a tame despair at the prospect of the difficulties before him, and throw away all the intelligence and thrift with which he may have been endowed, in the mere terror of the undertaking. The former course may involve him in inextricable disgrace and ruin : the latter dooms him to a chosen lethargy and want. As an illustration of the former, there was a young man tempted forward in apparently prosperous openings, who, though he never had two thousand pounds capital of his own, assumed a rent of more than half that sum for a desirable ware-house—allowed his family expenses to run up annually to five thousand more—traded in one year to an amount over one hundred and fifty thousand, and in a few years failed, leaving debts to the amount of fifty thousand pounds, of which he was never able to pay a single penny. Who could be surprised that his character was covered with dishonour, or that his conscience knew no real subsequent peace? He was prominent as a Christian man, but his haste to be rich, in this perplexity of his career, made shipwreck of his faith, and wrote upon his very countenance the deep lines of conscious wrong-doing which all might read. Yet there is surely here a middle path of industry, economy, and patient continuance in well-doing, which will lead a young man safely through this maze, and enable him to enjoy that accepting "blessing of God, which maketh rich, and addeth no sorrow therewith." Let him strive watchfully in this path, remembering that no man striving for the mastery can hope to be crowned except he strive lawfully. The richest inheritance which he can ever have on earth, and which he can never sacrifice or hazard with safety or hope, is the testimony of a good conscience before God, giving boldness to the countenance, elasticity to the spirit, and a conscious right to the confidence and respect of his fellow-men.

Added to these two perplexities, comes the constant increase of individual competition, from the multiplying of the numbers around the man of business who are engaged in similar occupations, and the necessary diminution of individual profits with which the business must in consequence be transacted by each. This is an inevitable result of the growing age and population of a country. Every class of human business in an old country becomes overstocked. The field of occupation is subdivided, until, in the business of life, as in the territory on which it is transacted, farms are cut up into acres, and acres into building spaces, and even these again compressed with an upward occupation of the sky above, in proportion as a possession of the area of the earth below is refused and unattainable. Such a separation of the parts of business, and such a competition between them, sharpens amazingly the powers of human invention. It has been the parent of all those thousands of machines by which the present age and our land are so distinguished, giving to one man the strength of hundreds, and accomplishing in hours the work of days. But it also almost equally forces the appetite, and what men will sometimes excuse as the necessity, for fraud. If machines are invented to supersede human labour by mechanical or brute force, and steam be made apparently to starve multitudes whose handiwork it displaces, so also must new plans of business be contrived, new agencies of enterprise be discovered, cheaper and more expeditious methods of accomplishment be invented, that by the products of advancing skill and better adapted intelligence competitors may be undersold, and the common business be carried on with increased advantage to the individual engaged. This competition is not to be avoided. When it is healthy and just it is not desirable that it should be. Its aggregate constitutes the wealth of a land, and its wholesome and stimulating operation promotes and secures the prosperity and comfort of multitudes who are not directly engaged in the circle of its contest. But it creates frequent and great perplexities to the individual trader, and often embarrasses and breaks down the young man of business in the beginning of his career. Frequently, also, there is great injustice perpetrated under the garb of just and equitable competition. A large trader with abundant capital will deliberately adopt the nature and occupation of the tiger among the flocks. Though already abundantly rich, and needing nothing more, he will devote himself to the oppressive persecution of competitors with smaller means. Instead of a noble and generous encouragement of them by maintaining the stand of the branch of trade in which they are engaged in common, he will undersell them even at a loss to himself. He will even ascertain the main staple of their investment, that he may especially destroy them by a ruinous reduction of the market price for this one class of merchandise. His purpose is no longer an honourable gain for himself, but a murderous ruin for others; and embarrassment and failure in trade, and hopeless debts, and secret family distress, and even heart-broken poverty and despairing suicide may be the results of this unrighteous oppression of the poor by the rich of this world. Such a man, while far from an advantage to the trade, is no benefit to the community in which he trades. Like some haughty and cruel landowners, who delight to sell out whole villages of the poor, to increase the area of their worthless parks, and to depopulate a neighbourhood by the grinding of the faces of the labouring and needy, till they compel hundreds to depart, that they may dwell alone, and that their game may roam where these poor ones were born, and where their fathers lie, and where they, too would willingly have toiled and died, and then affect to consider the splendour of their enlarged palaces, and the green silence of their outspread lawns, the index of the prosperity of the land which they have cursed, so does such an overgrown trader become the voluntary destroyer of hundreds, furnishing in return no increase to the common wealth, often even swearing out from just taxation for the public the whole amount of his ill-gathered property, and willingly sacrificing the happiness and prosperity of any and all others to his own selfish plans of covetous accumulation. This, in a greater or a less degree, is a frequent shape of the competition in which the man of business must contend. And when such a pressure comes upon one whose capital is small, and whose expenses are necessarily disproportionate to his means, the perplexity and the temptation are great, and the conscience and the stern purpose of honesty and right become often severely tried. The alternative frequently appears inevitable between absolute failure, with its painful results in poverty and domestic distress, and a sacrifice of truth and honesty, and the fear and favour of God, in unrighteous attempts for vindication and relief.

This increase of competition in trade necessarily also promotes the improvement of means and agencies for trade. And in this field again, while capital may be honourably invested, and skill and powers of invention may be justly and profitably employed, another contest is urged and maintained in which the want of capital is often the source of failure and ruin. A man may have invested his whole command of pecuniary ability in a style or method of operation of adequate and compensating profit, when the unexpected invention of machinery, or the discovery of some new principle of power by others, or their greater ability of capital for investment in such machinery or discovery, may instantly annihilate all his hopes of gain, and destroy the worth of all the investments which he holds. We cannot complain of this new element of contest, or righteously forbid its appearance and operation as a general fact in a community. The advance of the prosperity of the whole is, in such a case, more than a compensation for the losses of individuals. And the general prosperity of a community justly compels the claims of private interest and advantage to yield. It would be a mere absurdity to groan over the want of employment to individuals, however multiplied they are, which has followed from the amazing inventions of the steam-engine, the power-press, or the cotton-loom. Yet the fact has been equally real and pressing in a thousand cases of illustration. Each of these inventions threw multitudes out of work, and wrecked their little all in their unprovided voyage. And it required the endurance of much suffering, and the passage of a necessary interval of time, before the equilibrium was again restored, and the surrounding interests of individuals and the trade were once more adjusted. Such illustrations are likely always to occur. As advancing science brings its new discoveries to aid and adorn the arts, the mechanical and social powers of man must constantly increase; and the varieties of human invention will be multiplied in number, and carried further forward into the domains of actual work. Each new invention successfully operating both suggests the principle of another and excites to the effort for its realization. The skill of man is thus unceasingly sharpened and urged forward. A machine may be hardly a year old before some new discovery gets rid of its friction, or diminishes its expense, or reduces the cost of working it, and its doom is fixed. All its promises and hopes are compelled to yield to a more effective and successful competition. The reducing the price of manufacture of necessity regulates in its result the market for trade. And it is impossible to limit the field of application to which the process of invention may be carried. It is seen in all arts and preparations for navigation on the sea, and in all the schemes for mechanical power on the land. The lines and the materials of commerce, and the methods and courses of transportation are all in their turn involved. The man of business, to be a successful one, must be a quick, ready, intelligent, and thoroughly informed one, not only in the particular branch which he has selected, but in all the related and contingent branches which bear upon it; or the skill of invention will distance his powers, and the progress of discovery will leave him in the rear.

The possibility of this competition, or we might more justly say the certainty of it, in every shape and department of human trade, will be a frequent cause of new perplexity to the man of business. Wherever he may look around in a commercial community, whose free schools and active trade give every poor man's son the full chance for the exercise of all the powers with which God has endowed him, and urge him by every motive of hope, of gain, and of honour, to realize the wildest of his dreams of greatness and influence, this contest must grow more and more earnest and varied. And as the result, talent, industry, and enterprise, in their applications to the walks of trade, united with economy, honesty, and truth as the principles of its management, must be the occupants of the throne of social government, and rule and regulate the interests of individuals by the enlarging schemes which they propose. This whole inter-woven scheme of operation will enlarge and quicken the powers of every man of business, but it will also often exceedingly enhance and multiply the perplexities of his pursuit of trade.

All these perplexities come within the range of honourable traffic, and involve, in the general sources from whence they arise, nothing that is morally destructive. But beyond these, and perhaps occasionally connected with them all, there is the difficulty which arises from the prevalence of surrounding fraud in every branch of trade. The honest and upright man of business often finds himself placed in temporary disadvantage by the greater immediate facilities for success which others derive from a fraudulent pursuit of the same course of occupation. Destitute of conscience and honour, and indifferent to the law of God and the claims of truth, they can make false representations without hesitation, and take advantage of ignorance without remorse. The habits of deception often produce wonderful adroitness and skill in the management of the deceit. The alacrity of the pickpocket in the use of the nicely concealed knife in his finger-ring often renders him more than a match for any vigilance. The skill of the counterfeiter sometimes almost defies the most practised power of detection. And the unprincipled and violent portion of men seem for a season to triumph easily over the honest and the upright in their pursuit of the gains of earth. The likelihood of success appears thus to place a premium upon fraud. The contest between honesty and knavery, amidst the varied apparent disadvantages which attend upon the former, is often for a time extremely unequal. The upright man who struggles forward in the faithful and assiduous employment of his lawful and honourable opportunities for gain, resolving to maintain, in all his transactions, a conscience void of offence towards God and towards men, appears to have but little chance of success, in competition with a fraudulent neighbour, who buys without concern whether he shall ever pay, and borrows in enormous disproportion to his own ability, of the funds of others, reckless whether they shall ever be restored. To the one a failure, without the means to redeem the sacred pledges of his honest debts, is not only a dishonour in trade, but is also a violation of his own conscience of right—a result which inflicts far more pain upon a sensitive and upright mind than the mere pressure of outward disgrace. To the other the failure of payment is but a source of gain. He readily secrets from his creditors the stolen property in his possession, and settles his conscience and his debts at the lowest possible per centage of payment, and then chooses to represent himself as honourably discharged from obligation, and authorized to commence a new career with an entire oblivion of the past. A country merchant who had purchased a large amount of goods from some city houses failed in his payments, and made a proposition to his creditors for his release on their receipt of fifty per cent. of his obligations. The proposition was accepted, in ignorance of the real state of his affairs. He subsequently appeared at some of the same establishments to ask for a new credit, and when questioned as to his ability to pay, boldly alleged that he had now a handsome cash capital, for which he accounted in the statement that the assets in his hands from his former failure had turned out far better than he expected.   And all this advance he considered as a profit to which he was justly entitled, though there was still unpaid the half of every debt he owed before. The difficulties of active business in such circumstances of competition become very great.   The man of conscience, honesty, and truth must often be content with small gains during the period of such a contest, in the constant assurance of the compensating fact that the ultimate result of his operations will show him to have been no loser by his fidelity to truth and his maintenance of an incorruptible integrity in the sight of God.

These various perplexities of the man of business involve the pressure of increasing temptations to sacrifice the claims of honour and truth to the mere promises of a temporary expediency.   But let it never be forgotten that there is a principle of honour in the discharge of human business which beams with just as keen a defiance on the most accumulated power of temptation, and shines with an undimmed lustre in the most secret darkness of concealment.   There are men who shrink with a noble abhorrence from the contact of deceit, and turn their backs with instant loathing from all the delusive promises of ill-gotten gain.   They neither look upon the tempting cheat nor hearken to its most honeyed solicitations.   The in-

terests and property of others are as safe in their
hands as in the hands of the owners thereof.   Their
word of true and candid statement of facts realizes the
yea and nay of the divine description of truthful
communication.   Their promise is a sure security, and
those who rely upon them never find themselves
deceived.   Their friendship is the very soul of fidelity,
equally an honour and a pleasure to those to whom
it is extended.   Such men are the nobility of trade.
The community rejoice in their success, and multitudes partake of the benefits which flow from it.   In
influence, in example, and in direct efforts for the
welfare of their fellow-men, their intercourse with
others is like the genial dew of heaven, everywhere
descending, and descending only to fertilize and bless.
The walks of liberality are distinguished by their
presence; human wretchedness blesses their life; the
Church of God commemorates their benevolence ; and
science and literature, and all the great interests of
humanity and the public welfare, combine to acknowledge their merits and to enrol their reputation.
What an example and excitement are such competitors to the young and rising man of business!   And
how "like the shining light, which shineth more
and more unto the perfect day," is the path of
guidance and encouragement which they lay open,
and in which they walk!

But the perplexities of business often bear hard
upon this principle of unblemished and unrelaxing
honour, and men of feebler principles, and with a
conscience less stern in its demands, are in constant

danger of yielding to the evil influence, and of being carried away by the current of mere covetousness and love of the world. This principle of personal honour, of inherent and unchangeable integrity, is daily tried, and either becomes daily strengthened by a successful contest with temptation, or, yielding in little things, perishes by little and little; and many an Hazael who scorns the warning against possible crime, as an insult which reproaches him as if he were a dog, finds himself reduced by his heedlessness of the temptation to a condition of disgrace and ruin which dogs might pity. The first sacrifice of honour and truth in the walk of business is, as Solomon describes the starting of strife, "as when one letteth out water." It is a neglected chink in the dam; a leak which will hourly grow in its power and certainty of destruction; which is only to be met successfully when it is first discovered, or it will soon attain a power that will mock at vigilance and defy restrait.

The temptation comes in a thousand varied shapes, and no man of business, young or old, rich or poor, in trade, or profession, or handicraft, can feel himself exempted from its appearance or assured of security against its power. The sacrifice demanded is of this inward principle of conscience and truth in the sight of God. The prize which is offered is present immediate expediency and gain. The urgency to compliance is from the necessities of the condition, the difficulties of mere duty, the pressure of the perplexity of present circumstances, the impossibility of applying the principles of mere abstract morality to the exigencies of trade, the certainty that others will adopt the expedient proposed, the general employment of similar deceptions in the business of life, and finally, the alleged impossibility of transacting the business of the world in any other way. It seems to offer no other alternative than compliance with conscious falsehood and crime, or exclusion from the chosen walks of professional trade.

It may come in the shape of false representations of the value and usefulness of articles for sale, or of delusive trade in furnishing the materials which are desired and demanded. The specimen may be far better than the stock which it is claimed to represent, or the light in which an article is arranged, or the artificial and special advantage which is given to its appearance, may delude the purchaser into the bargain, while the seller triumphs in the gain which he has received, though perfectly conscious of the cheat and the loss which he has inflicted upon another. A young druggist of our acquaintance, whose conscience was quick in its sensitiveness to truth and honesty, once applied to an older Christian friend with the statement, " I am required to sell three different articles as medicines, under three different names, to purchasers who suppose them to be distinct things, and who buy them as such for distinct purposes. And yet I take them all out of the same vessel, and they are identically the same thing. How can I honestly practise a deception like this ? " And yet there seemed no way of escape but in the sacrifice of his place and all the advantages of his trade. A youthful assistant in a large grocery establishment once presented to us a similar case. "I am required to pack barrels of sugar with a small proportion of sugar of a finer quality at each end, and the whole of the centre filled up with an inferior kind; how can I do it?" Yet such an adulteration of goods, and such schemes of delusive trade, are so extensive that the honour and honesty of multitudes of our young men are destroyed in their mercantile education. Their integrity of heart and nature is ground completely out between the stones of example and necessity; and dishonest masters of trade thus inoculate their assistants with a *virus* too accordant with the selfish spirit of maturing man not to be effective and powerful in its influence upon their succeeding and independent life. But Christian integrity and honour can never sanction these false representations in traffic whether they are verbal or material. No authority or example can make them right, and no success or accumulation of gain can make them finally lucrative. There may be losses in the path of uprightness. The way of deception may seem right in a man's eyes for the occasion. Violence and dishonesty may banish the agent whose honour refuses compliance. But after all is done, it will be found better to have suffered for a season with a good conscience, than to increase our riches or maintain our stand in outward life by the perpetration of conscious crime. The man of business who has faithfully withstood this whole array of varied temptation, and who can survey all his gains as the gifts of God to his unwavering integrity, usefulness, and truth, will have an enjoyment in the retrospect of his days that prospered crime can never gain; while the divine testimony will be sustained by the whole history of human traffic, " He that getteth riches, and not by right, shall leave them in the midst of his days, and at his end shall be a fool."

Temptation comes also in the shape of a false representation of personal responsibility. The former course led to an unlawful accumulation by deceitful sale. This leads to the same result by a withholding of honourable and just obligations. Perhaps there is no shape in which the temptation to deception more habitually arises in business than this. It constantly occurs in a failure in trade—it comes in a false representation of the value and availability of assets; in the assertions of personal ability on the basis of which settlements with creditors are to be made; in the assumption of the sufficiency of a forced settlement as a legal and just discharge of the obligation of a debt. There is an habituation to this species of transaction in business, which makes it a subject of expectation when embarrassments and difficulties arise, and which almost blinds the conscience of the debtor to the reality and permanency of the obligation. But how can a man be honest in such a transaction? He compounds with a trusting creditor for ten per cent. perhaps, or fifty per cent. of his debt, often upon the basis of a false statement of his affairs; and thus holds himself honourably released. He subsequently engages in successful trade, or is employed in office at a large salary, or gains remuneration for some employment of talent or of time, and considers himself free and prosperous. He builds himself new houses; sets out with new furniture and display; and often meets the men whose hopes he has broken, and whose families he has ruined, with an unblushing front and a self-satisfied smile of welcome, while he honestly owes them it may be ninety per cent. of all their claim, with interest accruing. Can he be honest ? Can he be religious ? Is such a course to meet the approbation of upright men ? Can it ever deceive a God of truth and justice ? We answer, never. And every shilling that the man subsequently earns is the righteous property of others, until his whole obliga-tion is discharged. The Romans called debt *œs alienum*, which may be translated, "another man's money," or "stolen copper." Their rigid sense of justice would not allow that anything which the debtor held was his own. It was all "stolen copper." It must always be so. And no honourable or conscientious man can be satisfied until he has paid the uttermost farthing of his just obligations; and no position ought to give a man respectability among men, or restore the confidence of a community in his integrity, while he withholds from others the goods which are so justly and entirely their own. Most certainly all that he may thus appear to gain will be under the curse of emptiness of satisfac-tion and fickleness of possession in his future years. His money will be held in "a bag with holes;" and "the sweet remembrance of the just" can never adorn the record of his life.

The same temptation comes habitually in the dealings of the individual with the public. As a member of a community, the man of business owes "tribute to whom tribute is due; and custom to whom custom." His amount of obligation depends upon the value of the property which he holds. The social estimate of the value of his property must habitually rest upon their confidence in the truth of his own statement. It is fearful to think of the amounts and varieties of fraud which are practised under this one shape of an attempted escape from public burdens; the false oaths and deceitful statements which are made to avoid the impositions of the public revenue, the hiding of legal property from public taxation, and the deceitful statements which are made of the value of property legally assessed, to avoid the equitable impost thereon; so that fraudulent men of large possessions often entirely escape, and a disproportionate amount of taxation is thrown upon the honest and upright portion of the community, whose integrity and honour must be burdened to meet the frauds and deceptions of less conscientious men. We doubt whether any temptation to false representations in the pecuniary affairs of the community of business is more common than this. By some strange delusion in their medium of perception and calculation men often consider such frauds far less guilty than those which might occur in the mutual transactions of individuals. Many a man who could not be persuaded to swear falsely in a court of justice, or to utter a deliberate lie in private to his neighbour, or to steal from the property of another in the least amount, somehow finds his conscience far less imperative and strict when he deals with his country at a custom-house desk or the office of an assessor or receiver of taxes. But the purity of mercantile honour and the unvarying rule of Christian morality can never be made to depend upon the changing circumstances of individual relations. Truth and justice are eternal and unchangeable. Their claims alter with no circumstances. And no man can be in principle an honest or conscientious man who can make his own regard to their demands vary with the contingencies of his situation, or with the varying character of the persons with whom he deals. And the more pressing and habitual and undervalued is the kind of the temptation, the more circumspectly and sternly will the upright man of business resolve to walk in the strait and narrow way of perfect rectitude and unchanging truth.

The temptation which a life of business presents to an undue occupation of time must also be considered. The gain of wealth, and the transaction of the business which its varied employments demand, will always be a life of toil and labour. To take little rest and rise up early must be everywhere the habitual condition of its success. The combination of all the elements of perplexity in trade of which we have spoken bears upon this necessity for the increased and often excessive occupation of time. Family duties, relative domestic obligations, personal intellectual improvement, and all the refining relaxations of social life, are often sacrificed in this one pursuit of gain. The father and the husband lives in almost entire separation from the family whom he is bound to bring up for God, and

while he has been occupied in a fancied accumulation
for their benefit, the whole prospects and interests of
their character and welfare may have been made a
part of the price which he has paid for gain. It would
be well if this were all. But there is a deeper and
more precious interest still, which is just as habitually
sacrificed in the same course of trade. We speak of
the interests of the soul. Its hour of communion with
God in prayer—the morning and evening refreshment
of a labourer weary in his toil, and the rest of a pilgrim
in his daily journey—is carelessly thrown aside. It
becomes first formal and careless in the process of
this decay, and then ceases even in the form. The
Word of God, the great armoury of the Christian's
strength in the warfare of the earth, is neglected, laid
aside, and forgotten, till at last, in the regular and
unremitted descent of the soul from its high relations,
God is no more remembered, and the man learns to
live without him in the world. Easily, then, the time
of the six days' labour is found inadequate for the purposes which are proposed. The rest of the seventh is
coveted and stolen. When the soul is no longer alive
to God the repose of the Sabbath is transformed from
improvement to idleness. It may be that amusement
and dissipation will be seized upon as a means to hurry
its wearisome passage. The excess of the excitement
of the week is often found to make the quietness of the
Sabbath an intolerable contrast; and the man whose
nervous system has been on the stretch in all the preceding days of toil, finds himself perfectly languid and
wretched unless he can, by some varying of the earnest-

ness of occupation, keep up the unnatural and over-
wrought condition.   The home is deserted, the church
despised, and the roadside tavern or the noisy joviality
of some country assembly, of similar tastes and habits,
is made the substitute for that heavenly rest in social
life which the Lord, who made the Sabbath for man,
has appointed as his "tired nature's sweet restorer."
The excess of the weekly labour becomes a sufficient
excuse for the Sabbath idleness ; or the Sabbath desecration becomes a part of the price which deluded man
is tempted to pay for gain.   Often the same cause
demands also the employment of the Sabbath in the
continuance of the weekly labour; and the hours of
God's holy time are robbed for the writing up of books
or the maintenance of a correspondence for which no
adequate time is found beside.   The divine command
is nothing.   The welfare of the soul is nothing.   The
hopes of the future world are nothing.   The religious
life and character of a family are nothing.   The tra-
ditional effect of example is nothing.   The holiness and
happiness of the community are nothing.   But gain is
everything.   And the man of business finds the temptation press him on every side to make his gold his
god, the present world his all, and earthly accumulation
the Moloch to whom he makes at last the ready and
cheerful holocaust of all that is dignified in his nature,
happy in his condition, or hopeful in his prospects.
And what has he gained when God takes away his
soul ?   His birthright sold for a mess of pottage—his
blessing bartered for an hour's enjoyment, or a life with
no enjoyment—his hope in God sacrificed for gains

which have perished in the using—and himself left to
the prospect of a gloomy and unprovided departure—a
dying hour with no comfort or hope; while of all that
he hath gained he can carry nothing away with him,
but naked as he came must he also go, and look forward
to an account before a Being whose eyes of truth will
not be mocked, and who cannot be deceived.

Are such sacrifices as these demanded by a life of
business? May not man fill up the measure of his
personal and relative responsibility at a price less than
this? Has his Creator placed him where he cannot be
honest without ruin or prosper without crime? Let
us go back to our first and fundamental principles.
Life must be regarded in its real character and relations;
and the comparative value of the objects for which it
was given be justly and proportionately valued.

> " It is not all of life to live,
> Nor all of death to die."

There is something in the life more than meat, and in
the body more than raiment, and this invaluable something, this heavenly trust, with all its issues and
responsibilities, must be kept in view. There is a soul
which God hath loved, which his Son hath redeemed,
which his Spirit would sanctify, and for which he has
prepared an inheritance incorruptible in the heavens.
It must never be forgotten. Sin is its destruction:
and sin is to be measured, not by the ways and thoughts
of man, but by the law of God. Life is the scene and
place of the education and trial of this immortal soul
in preparation for an eternal being. Every lawful

occupation of man is the appointed place in which this education and trial are individually to be carried out, and every act or duty which makes up a part of that occupation exercises an undying influence upon the destinies and hopes of this immortal being. Thus must man estimate, and thus must he regard the elements of his condition here, the portions of his lot on earth. Every hour and every act may be a step onward to his crowning glory. Every occurring perplexity is an appointed test of his faith and his obedience. Every changing relation is bringing out a new aspect of his progressive tuition and exercise, and each day as it passes he is laying up the foundation against the time to come, either of increasing virtue, that has contended without injury through its successive trials, or of vain and deluding selfishness, which will leave him helpless, and empty, and despairing in the end. By all the value of these imperishable interests, and by all the dangers and contests to which they are exposed, would we entreat the young man of business to use the world as not abusing it; to make the tried and unchanging Word of God his constant guide, bringing every gain, every employment, and every temptation to its holy and unrelaxing standard; and so to press onward through all the cares and temptations of his varied life, that they shall all be made to stand as living witnesses of his proved fidelity before the judgment-seat of an unchangeable and compensating God.

MEN OF BUSINESS:

THEIR INTELLECTUAL CULTURE.

---◆---

JONATHAN F. STEARNS, D.D.

MEN OF BUSINESS:

THEIR INTELLECTUAL CULTURE.

INTELLIGENCE is an essential requisite to right action. It is the source of power. It serves to develop and advance to their proper maturity all the faculties with which God has endowed us. It is the nurse and instrument of virtue. It is the handmaid of religion. We can scarcely over-estimate it, though we may assign to it a disproportionate value; and this we shall do if we exalt it above moral and religious attainments, or admit that it can accomplish much good, either for individuals or for the community, when these are neglected.

But the cultivation of the intellect, based upon moral and religious principles, and subordinate to them, exalts our nature and enlarges all our capacities for enjoyment and usefulness. It is not the privilege only of the few. In different degrees, varying according to capacity and circumstances, it is the common boon of humanity. All classes ought to be admitted to its benefits. And yet it cannot be denied that they especially require and are entitled to them on whom devolve the leading parts in the great drama of human action and advancement.

The social state requires for its well-being a great variety of services. Society is not a mere aggregation, a quantity to be estimated by the relations of more and less, or better and worse, but an organic whole— a system in which the individuals are all members, each needful for each, and all for all. A heap of grain may be larger or smaller. A bag of money may contain a greater or less number of coins, and these may be severally of greater or less value. Take one away and there is but just so much less remaining. But it is not so with human society. That resembles rather an engine or a watch. Every wheel or spring or valve has its appropriate use. A thousand pistons could not supply the place of one safety-valve, nor a thousand mainsprings that of one balance wheel.

In a low state of civilization the diversities of employment are comparatively few. Men's habits are simple, and they have few wants. But as improvement advances, wants multiply. The demand for superior products creates a necessity for more concentrated application. Society gets distributed into various classes, each occupying its own allotted sphere, and doing its own work, with an exclusiveness which, at first view, seems totally indifferent to the pursuits of others. And yet, if you look narrowly, that very exclusiveness shows the existence of a most extensive and closely connected inter-dependence.

In such a system no one of the legitimate employments can well be dispensed with. There are, it is true, vicious employments and vicious distinctions in society, whose continuance and success we cannot but regard with dread. They are the evil growth of a diseased state of the body politic. Plato thought it wise to exclude from his theoretic commonwealth several arts and professions which, in the present state of the world, are held in high esteem. So would the Christian statesman, looking over the community as it now is, see occasion to depreciate and discourage not a few which hold a place among us only as the instruments of men's vices. But not of this character are those various trades, professions, or vocations by which virtuous men obtain their livelihood—those, namely, which supply some real want, avert some dreaded evil, or promote some valuable improvement of humanity. These may be looked upon as but so many limbs or organs of the body politic—instruments of its wellbeing or well-working. Take any of them away, and what remains is not merely a diminished quantity, but a disordered, maimed, and crippled whole. Our civilization—to wit, such civilization as Christian influences have developed—requires for its support and advancement just such branches of physical and mental industry as we see flourishing around us. And it is a matter of interest to the entire community, not only that each class should be sustained, but that to each should be given the best possible training to fit them for their several callings.

Among these classes stands prominent THE MAN OF BUSINESS. In claiming for him a large share of intellectual culture we have regard to the important character of his functions, and the leading position which he is to occupy among the forces of society.

We include in this class not the merchant or the trader only, though these may be regarded as the type of the class,—they are its most prominent specimens, and the pursuits of the man of business, in all departments, partake more or less of the mercantile character : we include in it all those whose vocation it is to organize and direct the industrial forces of the community—the manufacturer, the master mechanic, the contractor, or the superintendent, in the various enterprises of production, accommodation, or improvement. All our higher wants require complicated processes and combined skill. The man of business undertakes to bring about the requisite combination— to afford facilities for it, and to furnish to the various classes of society, each according to their wants, the finished results.

To this class every other in the community is a debtor. The labourer, the artizan, the artist, the traveller, the statesman and jurist, the clergyman, the physician, the devotee of science, and the man of literary leisure—what could any of them accomplish but for the reliance they are allowed to place on the skill, energy, activity, and faithfulness of the man of business? His enterprises furnish employment to thousands who could not otherwise have employed themselves; and the little dowry and patrimony on which the widow and orphan rely for their daily bread finds its entire productive value in the profitable uses to which he is able to apply it. His class forms the very sinews, ligaments, and conducting arteries of all social organization. He acts as mediator between the individual and the community, and by his agency alone the possessions, talents, and achievements of one acquire a real value for all.

We are looking with great interest to the improvement of society. But there has never been any considerable social advancement, whether in ancient or modern times, wherein this class has not first or last played a prominent part. China and India, as their earliest records show, distinguished themselves as mercantile nations from the earliest antiquity. Assyria, Phœnicia, Carthage suggest the idea of commercial greatness on the bare mention of their names. One of the earliest notices we have of ancient Egypt is that of companies of merchants travelling from Gilead, to bring "spices, myrrh, and balm," and carry them down thither as articles of traffic. Greece, the most accomplished of the ancient nations, owed all her great superiority, her laws, her commanding influence among the nations, her philosophy, her refinement in art, literature, and manners, in no small degree to the stimulus given to her once rude people by commercial enterprises. These old heathen civilizations, such as they were—and none can doubt they were a great improvement on the barbarism that preceded and surrounded them—grew up, not so much under the shades of leisurely contemplation, as in the dust and stir and jostling competition of business. And the nation of Israel—though their civilization was designed to bear a peculiar character, less dependent than that of others upon this class of influences—show plainly, in the days of their greatest prosperity and glory—the days of Solomon—a very remarkable development of business enterprise and activity.

If we turn to the civilization of modern times we find there a very marked illustration of the point before us. It took its beginnings amidst scenes of violence and confusion. The wreck of former grandeur and opulence was strewed over the waves of centuries. The providence of God, having in view some better product, had broken up all the old systems of social organization, and ground them into shapeless masses, so as to prepare them to receive a new principle. There they lay, heaving and fermenting over an entire continent. Business men, at that period, scarcely existed as a class. War exhausted the talents, the energies, and the resources of the superior classes, and hopeless servitude was the fate of the inferior. The feudal chieftain, the successful soldier, and the wily ecclesiastic, held in their own hands the forces of the world, and dealt out its resources as they chose to their dependent retainers. Then the intercourse of nations did not lie in the exchange of commodities. The gathering of wealth was a matter of wholesale robbery or of cunning extortion. The banker was a Jew; the lender of money was a usurer; the merchant was regarded as one who extorts a kind of tribute from the luxury or necessities of his fellow-men. And hence we find, among the acts of ecclesiastical councils—those most potent engines of power in the Middle Ages—a decree condemning the employment of the merchant, as one which no virtuous Christian could pursue.

But the fabric of society could not always remain in this confused and broken state. A principle was at work tending to reorganize it on a nobler plan. Christianity began to work its way among the social elements; and now the appropriate agent of advancing civilization began anew to acquire dignity and import- ance. Business became an essential function of the social system. The earth was found to contain inex- haustible riches fitted to man's use, intellectual and physical. Princely magnificence did not comprise all the magnificence of the world. The cabinets of kings did not contain all the gems, nor their treasuries all the silver and gold, nor the rich cathedrals of those other lords, the rulers of the Church, all the marbles and precious stones, nor the broad lands seized by the swords of the one or given to the other as the bribe of salvation—all the productive soil given to man by the divine bounty as his ample inheritance. Caravans crossed the desert, and came back loaded with the wealth of distant India—gold and gems from its mines, pearls from its oceans, sweet odours from its forests, silk from its looms. Adventurous mariners pushed their way over unknown seas, and opened new chan- nels for the intercourse of traffic. They crossed the wild and hitherto mysterious ocean, and added new lands— a new world, as it was appropriately called—to the habitable earth known to their fathers—lands richer than fable, and beautiful, even in their native wildness, as the garden of Eden. To bring these new lands into use and occupancy, to develop and apply to useful pur- poses resources which had been locked up since crea-

tion, to make the superfluity of one land supply the
deficiencies of another, to increase wealth as well as to
make it exchange hands, to make money as well as to
get it, now woke into the most eager exercise powers
and faculties which had hitherto lain dormant. Thus
cities rose. Freedom was felt as a necessity, and was
claimed and vindicated as a right. Invention was
stimulated, art began to put forth her beautiful creations, knowledge increased, genius and talent were
called forth, civilization advanced.

When we look back over a period of five hundred
years and compare, or rather contrast, the condition
of the world then and now, how great is our astonish-
ment!   And what. has accomplished this change?
science? art? general intelligence? free government?
Yes ; all these unquestionably have had their influence.
But there has been another force steadily operating,
without whose aid and instrumentality none of these
could have accomplished what they have done.   It is
trade. This has given to science one of its most
effective stimulants. It has been an engine of freedom,
undermining feudalism, diffusing intelligence, elevating
the people. Religion owns its services, and has found
in it a most effective instrument for its purposes.
The Reformation, humanly speaking, could not have
taken place without it ; the standard of the cross,
waving benignly amidst Christian homes and the rich
products of Christian civilization, could not have been
erected on these new shores ; nor could Christian
missionaries, bearing messages of salvation, have gone
forth into the four corners of the earth.

From these facts it has followed as a matter of course that the class of men engaged in managing this agency have assumed a very different position from that which they once occupied. History tells us how it was at a very early day. The Medici of Florence, those merchant princes, whose financial operations controlled the march of armies, and made and unmade kings—whose palaces were the seat, not of wealth and power only, but of taste, of art, of refinement, of all sorts of intellectual culture—were but a prominent specimen, among many who filled the cities of Italy with learned men, and wrote chapters in the book of history, over which modern eyes linger with admiration. Nor was it their riches only that gave them this elevation. It was the functions they discharged. The baron and the king, the bishop and the pope, saw a mighty rival—not in respect to wealth and splendour only, but to power, to control over the actions and destinies of men, to whatsoever gives authority and dignity to man in the eyes of his fellows—in the owner of rich argosies. Awhile they strove to patronize the new nobility, give to a few of its chiefs a certain place in their own ranks, and make it receive at their hands its privileges and honours. Hence merchants became princes, and merchants' sons generals, prime ministers, or high ecclesiastics. But this could not last always. The new power was not long a child. It had a giant's strength and a giant's proportions. There was in it a spirit not of independence only, but of authority. Gradually it won its way against the opposing force of older dynasties, fighting and yielding, fighting and yielding under the pressure of influences long dominant, until at length it became an established and well-recognized power among the nations; and, taking its seat side by side with the most legitimate, sways a sceptre which not a government in the world would venture to disregard.

Were the question asked, What is at this moment the strongest power in operation for controlling, regulating, and inciting the actions of men? what has most at its disposal the condition and destinies of the world? We must answer at once, it is that business, in its various ranks and departments, of which commerce, foreign and domestic, is the most appropriate representation. In all prosperous and advancing communities—advancing in arts, knowledge, literature, and social refinement—business is king. Other influences may be equally indispensable, and some may think far more dignified, but business is king. The statesman and the scholar, the nobleman and the prince, equally with the manufacturer, the mechanic, and the labourer, pursue their several objects only by leave granted and means furnished by this potentate.

And if this is true as a characteristic of the age generally, it is pre-eminently so of our own country; because, it being a new country, all that is valuable in it is pre-eminently in a progressive state. We have our fortunes yet to make, intellectually and socially, as well as physically. Our mansions are to be built, our institutions founded, our facilities of intercourse perfected, our treasures dug out of the earth, and all the resources of the land discovered and developed. You may set a soldier

to guard an old cabinet of crown-jewels, valued chiefly
as the relics of ancient kings; or you may lock them up
in a strong box, and enclose them within the massive
walls of a strong castle; but it requires enterprise, systematic and well-organized industry, and the skill and
courage to lay *out*, as well as to lay *up*, in order to
discover, bring forth, and mould into new forms of
beauty, the riches which lie hid where God hoarded
them, in the jewel-cabinets and treasuries of nature.
Old conservatism, looking only to the past, may afford
to dispense with business, and perhaps affect to despise
it, but young and hopeful progress never.   In such a
country as ours business must stand in relations of
peculiar intimacy with every pursuit and calling that
deserves a place in the social economy.   Even the
products of the mind—ideas, principles, sentiments,
moral and religious truths—if ever they are to become
parts of the common inheritance, working forces in the
action of the community, elements of its character, and
guides of its life, must make their way to such commanding influence under its banner.   You cannot
build a school-house or a college, you cannot publish a
book, without its intervention.   The book must be one
that will sell, or who does not know that, for all the
purposes for which books are intended, it might just
as well not have been written?   A pulpit cannot be
maintained without the same agency.

Now, from all these considerations, who does not
perceive the vast importance of looking well to the
character, intellectual as well as moral and religious, of
our business men?   They constitute a claim on their

behalf to a high order of intellectual attainments. That a class occupying so leading a position, managing interests of such vast importance, and standing in such vital relations to the community and the age, should be a mere race of drudges, incompetent to understand their own position, and the significance of their own operations, is a disgrace and wrong not to be tolerated. We have said, business is king. A burning shame would it be, in such an age as this, that the ministers who stand by the throne and execute the behests of this sovereign should be any other than intelligent men. Narrow and low views, vulgar conceptions, ignorance of the true nature and destiny of mankind, and of the great principles of truth and righteousness which ought to govern the world, if they prevail here, will be sure to extend their influence, to the corruption and degradation of the entire community. No learned class, no efforts either of the pulpit or the press, could do more than check the progress of deterioration against such influences.

We have been looking hopefully for a higher type of manhood to rise among us, under the influence of a purer and more fully developed Protestant Christianity. " The age of chivalry," said an illustrious British statesman, "is gone." Gone it is; you can never recall it. Society has taken a new shape, and the energies of the race have passed over into a new field. But what if, with the more sterling and practical virtues which seem naturally to belong to this field, we could reproduce, and that in a purer form, the very qualities that gave attractions to the old—the bloom, and verdure, and

freshness of the ancient knighthood in the quiet
measured gardens of modern industry and enterprise?
Are war, and lawless violence, and the semi-barbarous
relations of lord and vassal, really a better state for the
development of some of the nobler virtues of humanity
than peace, order, social equality, and the pursuits of
industry? Then has the Gospel of peace left defects
in the culture which it offers, to be supplied only by its
antagonist! Then the wolf must not always and everywhere dwell with the lamb, nor the leopard lie down
with the kid! We shall be very slow to admit such a
conclusion. We venture, on the contrary, to affirm
that all that heroic energy, that courageous prudence,
that independent deference, that self-reliant self-devo-
tion, that high integrity, " that sensibility of principle,
that chastity of honour which felt a stain as a wound,"
so eminently characteristic of the ancient chivalry in
its best specimens, may be reproduced on an improved
plan, in what are deemed by many the dull, unpoetical,
and selfish walks of a life of business; yes, even " the
unbought grace of life, the cheap defence of nations, the
nurse of manly sentiment and heroic enterprise," in
an age and nation of " economists, calculators, and
shopkeepers."

But if this be true, if the very thought be not a
romantic dream, the result can only be accomplished by
elevating the character, intellectual as well as moral
and religious, of our men of business. Fortunately we
have some noble examples of what may be accomplished
in this respect. But these examples must be emulated
to a degree far surpassing what we have hitherto wit-

nessed. Our business men must feel it to be not their privilege only, but their sacred duty, to cultivate their minds and furnish them, in as large measures as possible, with the pleasures and advantages of knowledge.

As to the direct preparation of the man of business for the duties of his calling, some may doubt whether intellectual culture, properly so called, is of any material importance. Leave that, they say, to scholars, to men of leisure, to the learned professions. Business is a practical matter: it requires experience rather than study. The sharpening of the faculties by exercise, the skill and insight which are derived from the actual doing of the work, the training afforded by the homely and practical duties of an apprenticeship, are worth more to the formation of a good business character than all the studies of the school or the college. And possibly this is true, if we must speak comparatively —if we must choose one of the two and dispense with the other. There are certain parts of the business man's duties, certain details, a certain routine, the qualification for which can be obtained only in the shop or counting-house. And these qualifications are indispensable; they must be acquired so thoroughly as to become a matter of habit. But this is equally true, though perhaps in a less degree, in what are called the learned professions. The young lawyer must have an office-training as well as a school-training. The young physician must attend at the hospitals or visit the houses of the sick in company with his teacher, as well as attend courses of lectures at the medical college. But if, in these latter cases, theory is necessary in order to illuminate and guide practice; and practice, in order to be successful, must consent to be the executor of a well-studied theory, so in the former. There are theoretic truths applicable to business; there are principles, there are fixed and general laws, determining its aims and regulating its processes, just as truly as in matters usually denominated scientific. The man who is capable of reflection, of induction and deduction, who has facts wisely gathered in his possession, and can see their bearings and relations, who understands general principles and is able to apply them in all exigencies, must have an immense advantage, even in the common matters of gain and loss, over the man of blind processes and stereotyped maxims.

It is very true that many a learned man has utterly failed in the attempt to be a man of business. And, on the other hand, many an ignorant man has had what has been deemed great success in conducting extensive business operations, and amassing property. Some examples of the latter sort are familiar in story. In a small but flourishing seaport of New England there lived, fifty years ago, a man so ignorant that he could not spell correctly the commonest words in his language. All his acquaintance regarded him as only half-witted, although the wit he had was, in some of its characteristics, peculiarly shrewd. This man amassed a fortune. Whatever he touched turned to a profit; and even his most ridiculous blunders were among his most productive speculations. We have all heard of, or been acquainted with, cases of the same sort, only perhaps less marked. But these are mere matters of accident. They are not examples to be imitated. Men have won fortunes many a time in a lottery; but that does not show that chance is the best reliance in accumulating property. According to all experience, she cheats her votaries far oftener than she prospers them.

We readily admit that the department of business is among the most practical of all the departments of life. Without insight, experience, systematic habits, and practical energy, a man is totally disqualified for its duties. And yet this does not hinder us from believing that the man who superadds to all these qualifications study and thought is better qualified, even for the most practical of these duties, than he who dispenses with them.

There is a vast extent and variety of knowledge which may be made directly available, first or last, in business operations. Profit and loss are often determined by it. A man, for example, is engaged in supplying some one or more of the wants of mankind. He needs to know what those wants are; in what circumstances they arise; which among them are permanent, and which of a temporary nature; in regard to the latter, in what circumstances they are likely to cease, or what may turn them aside into some new channel; how far he may or may not count upon the continuance of their demands amidst the fluctuations of the times; what articles are best suited to the supply in the particular locality which he has selected for his operations; where the best and most suitable of those articles can be most advantageously secured; what quantity is required; what the fluctuations are to which the price may be subject; the physical influences to which they are liable, either for deteriorating or improving the value; how long they may be allowed to lie on hand without danger of loss; to what degree he may safely extend his transactions with the amount of capital he is able to command; what are the approved rules of intercourse between the buyer and the seller, or the dealer in wholesale and retail; the laws of the land affecting such transactions as his own; and what changes in the public policy, either of his own or other countries, are likely to promote or thwart the success of his undertakings. Questions of this nature may be multiplied to almost any extent, in connection with the simplest operations. And they run out, as may be seen at a glance, into almost every department of knowledge—to history, to geography, to natural science, to political economy, to mercantile ethics, to finance, to jurisprudence, to politics. He who has made himself acquainted with these matters— who has no occasion to go and study them out, or to depend upon the opinion of others, or guess the result which he would ascertain from such vague signs as he may be able to discover, or run his risk and take his chance for want of power to form an intelligent opinion —has an advantage, even on the direct question of gain or loss, of no mean value to its possessor.

But to this, perhaps, some one will reply: Oh! I cannot take time to go into all these considerations; I must follow my practical judgment. I judge of the goodness of an article by its look, its taste, its smell; I judge of the profitableness of buying and selling by inquiring into the state and tendencies of the market; I get a habit of judging. Yes; but suppose you might obtain the power to judge where the habit and the signs would not serve you. Suppose you could anticipate the state of the market—anticipate all its apparent tendencies—by a true knowledge of the causes to which all its variations are subject. You need not take time in order to put this knowledge into use. If it is really yours it will come to the aid of your practical judgment just as readily as the knowledge furnished by experience. You spend time now; you stop, and hesitate, and inquire, and after all get deceived in your conclusions, when, if you only had at your command such knowledge as we are now recommending, a simple glance at the newspaper, or the slightest consideration of the signs of the times, might have enabled you to determine the question at once, and that with decision and certainty.

But if these remarks may be applied to the more simple and limited departments of the pursuits in question, how much more when we come to the more extensive and complicated—to commerce in the larger sense—to the operations of the importer, of the banker, of the manager of large manufacturing interests. When we consider how these operations spread themselves over the world, and are connected, either directly or indirectly, with all its interests, experiences, and events—that a revolution in China, a failure of the opium crop in India, or the cotton crop in the United

States, the embarrassment of financial affairs in France or England, the curtailment or expansion of a banking-house three hundred miles off, the tone and temper of a speech in the British Parliament, a change in the tariff, the annexation or organization of a new territory, the opening of a new channel of communication, the chartering or refusing to charter a new railroad, may make the difference of success or failure, prosperity or ruin; that all these events are to be anticipated, provided for, and turned to account—the range of knowledge of which men engaged in such pursuits find it convenient to avail themselves seems scarcely to admit of a limitation.

We do not forget, indeed, that even the most extensive business has its own department or specialty, to which the knowledge necessary for its management may be thought chiefly to be limited. But then no department, however narrow it may seem, is without its relations. And if those relations are not understood —if the collateral departments on which they hinge are not taken into the account—a man is in no condition to conduct well even the most limited specialty. Every man's own particular path must be the middle line of his knowledge; and subjects which lie contiguous to it form the foreground of the picture which he is to study; but then there is a background altogether essential to the character and completeness of the whole, which stretches far away in every direction to unlimited distances.

We have spoken thus far of knowledge, and that with reference to its immediate uses. But this is but a partial view of the matter. The man of business, especially in its higher departments, needs to possess a well-furnished, well-disciplined, and well-cultivated mind.

The object of education is not by any means chiefly the use to which the acquirements of the student are to be directly put. Why is the young aspirant for the profession of law kept in school and college, studying year after year dead languages and abstract problems in mathematics? Not because he is expected to use the one in his professional intercourse or the other in calculating professional questions. A large part of what he learns may be forgotten presently, as to any use which he has to make of it. It has done its work in the very getting of it; in the fact that it has once been in the mind, and left its impress upon other faculties besides the memory—upon the judgment, upon the power of abstraction and reasoning, upon the capacity for acquiring other knowledge hereafter to be learned. And as for the rest, by far the larger part has only an indirect bearing upon practical matters. Education aims chiefly at the formation of the mind itself. It has its chief use, so far as practical matters are concerned, in the fact that a mind well trained and well informed acts with the more power, certainty, and effect, upon whatsoever particular object its faculties are exerted.

Now the pursuits of the man of business, at least in the higher departments, require a wide range of high mental qualifications. He must have energy, activity, promptness, regularity, system, punctuality, exactness, decision, self-reliance, penetration, integrity, honour.

And these are qualities, practical as they may seem, which are greatly promoted, every one of them, by a careful training of the mental faculties. Some of them are the very same which the scholar by profession aims most assiduously to acquire—the very same, indeed, for which the course of studies usually dignified with the name of liberal was designed.

Besides, the value of such studies to this class of men, in enlarging the field of intellectual vision, can hardly be exaggerated. The world itself is a very different thing to the man of learning from what it is to the ignorant. The relations which the one sees in it are broad as the canopy of heaven ; while to the other everything is isolated, and he sees nothing but what meets his outward eye. While the latter fixes his attention on a single point, and is confined to that, the former radiates his views all round it, and sees in intimate connection with it every other in the wide universe of space and time.

This comprehensiveness of vision the man of business needs in a high degree. The wide and complicated relations of his vocation, and the liability of his conclusions to be vitiated by a slight mistake in any one of a thousand particulars, indispensably require it. He must adhere diligently to his own proper employment, refusing, doggedly almost, to be turned aside from it to the right hand or the left. But he must be able to look, as with the keen eye of the eagle and the quickness of the lightning's flash, on every side at once, and to the remotest distances. Staying constantly at home, occupying as it were, year after year, the same spot at the same desk, his mind must have its couriers coursing through the world and its posts hastening to and fro to bring and bear intelligence between the remotest corners of the domain of knowledge. Nor is this all. He needs to be what has been called a *many-sided* man. With a comprehensiveness which can grasp at once the sum total of the most complicated problems, he must be able to combine the minutest attention to even fractional details; with a spirit of enterprise which springs at once to results, and grasps success, a patience which is willing to take every intermediate step; with a boldness which trifles cannot intimidate, nor accidental reverses discourage, a caution which looks to all the probabilities and chances of the case in hand, carefully counting the cost.

And is it reasonable to suppose a mind, possessing such capacities, at once so telescopic and so microscopic, can be formed without careful training and a large share of intellectual culture? Is it a fruit that ordinarily grows wild upon the stock of humanity? We do not say that no man is fit to be a man of business who has not enjoyed what is commonly called a liberal education; but we do say that an education based upon the same principles, having reference chiefly to the enlarging, furnishing, and disciplining of the mind itself, would, if rightly directed, be of vast benefit to men of this class, with at least an indirect reference to the particular duties of their vocation. Some such broad, and yet exact and systematic, culture seems indispensable, in order to give them the required mental qualities. They must be trained to steady thought. They must be made to possess the full and free use of all their faculties and powers. They must be in readiness for an incalculable variety of unanticipated exigencies. And for this end no narrow and superficial education will suffice. They must have much and hard study. Science, literature, and art must at least have *introduced* them to their ample stores; and what they do not know, in any department of the field of knowledge, they must at least have learned where to search for, and by what methods to obtain it. No mere routine of practice, however familiar; no professional education, however thorough; no system of rules, however excellent, will give a man the same advantage. He must know a great deal more than he wants to use in his profession; he must have exercised his mind on subjects with which his business has nothing to do, or it is impossible that he should ever possess it.

The attainment of as large a share as may be practicable of intellectual culture is a duty which every man of business owes to his profession. It is to the want of it that we must ascribe the prevalent low views concerning the proper aims and ends of business pursuits. Many, for example, have no conception of the profession of the merchant but as a method of accumulating property; nor of commerce, even in its widest scope, but as a speculation upon chances. The philosopher professes to devote his powers to the enlightenment of mankind; the statesman understands that the interests of a nation are entrusted to his charge; the lawyer knows that, besides the obtaining of his fees, he has a solemn responsibility laid upon him to see that the rights of his client, who might otherwise suffer wrong, are properly vindicated; the minister of the Gospel dares not enter upon his profession, nor think of his salary, without professing, not to his fellow-men only, but to his own conscience, that he is moved by a supreme desire to serve God, promote virtue and piety, and save the immortal souls of his fellow-men. True, they have all in view the obtaining of a livelihood—some of them the amassing of wealth : they pursue this object often with more than justifiable eagerness ; but they understand perfectly that, as a matter of morality, it is to be kept subordinate to other and higher objects of their calling. A man's reputation as a lawyer does not depend upon the rapidity with which he gets rich by his profession. His getting rich may or may not depend upon the ability with which he defends his clients; but it is the latter only, not the former, which forms the basis of his reputation. In the case of the man of business, how frequently is all this simply reversed! Ask him what is the object of his business, and he will tell you, with an unconscious frankness almost ludicrous, that it is to *make money*. He is a conscientious man, perhaps. He means to do all honestly. He scorns to take an undue advantage or transgress any of the rules of fair and honourable traffic. But the getting of money is his grand object. In proportion as he gets money he regards his business as successful, and in proportion as he fails in that, all his operations seem a failure. Thus is the lust of gain, that characteristic vice of the mercantile world, stimulated to an absorbing passion, and exalted almost to the rank of a virtue. The constant inquiry is how he shall increase what he denominates his worth. He struggles to attain now this mark, and now that, in the ascending scale of accumulation, until the passion, gaining strength by indulgence, eats out the very life of the soul, and dries up all the fountains of noble feeling and desire.

But we see not what there is in the true nature and ends of the business vocation to justify so debasing a conception. We admit that wealth stands in closer relation to this branch of human activity than to some others, because capital is one of the main instruments of commerce. But aside from this, we see not how it is any more a legitimate end here than in any other pursuit. Business is an important function of society. The man who engages in it accepts a trust. He works for you, for me, for the king on his throne, for the poor widow in her little apartment, for the student in his study, and the traveller in his distant journeys. His aim should be, chiefly, to discharge his trust well, and so to benefit the world. It is just as sordid, just as reprehensible for him to be thinking merely of his gains, as for the scholar, the teacher of science, or even for the Christian minister. And yet, such are the notions that prevail, that, while every other profession must talk of their gains with bated breath, the man of business puts them forth in the front ranks, and glorifies himself before the world on account of them.

All this results, we apprehend, in no small degree from the low state of intellectual culture with which the class in question have in general been satisfied. It is not due simply to low morality, for there is, we believe, as high moral principle here as elsewhere. But it is to be attributed to a want of that broad and liberal education which, by embracing at a single view the world and all its vast and complicated relations, would enable them to appreciate the true dignity and high public importance of a vocation connected, either directly or indirectly, with all the interests of mankind.

The attainment of such culture the man of business owes likewise to himself. Next to the satisfaction of an approving conscience, and of a sense of peace with God, there is no enjoyment of which the mind is capable more pure and satisfying than that which springs from the appropriate exercise of the intellectual faculties in the study and contemplation of God's works. As an old Roman has very justly observed, "These studies nourish our youth and delight our old age; they adorn our prosperity, and are a refuge and solace in adversity; they please us at home, and are no encumbrance abroad; they abide with us by night, accompany us on our journeys, and employ us in our country retirement." Newton's nervous excitement, when the proof of his new theory of gravitation dawned upon him in the distance; Pythagoras's hecatomb, offered up as a thanksgiving sacrifice to the gods, when the solution of a long-studied geometrical problem was discovered. The shout of Archimedes, "Eureka!

Eureka! I have found it! I have found it!" as, forgetting all proprieties of place and circumstances in his
eager joy at a scientific discovery, he rushed naked out
of the bath—are illustrations of the intensity of these
pleasures. The conqueror amidst the shouts of an
admiring nation was never more delighted than were
these conquerors in the battle-fields of knowledge.
And if this be so, who has a better right to partake of
the gratification; who has more need of the refreshment and exhilaration of soul to be derived from at
least sipping at the pure and healthful fountains of
literature and science, than he who is compelled to
drudge all day, in dust, and noise, and confusion,
among loaded drays and heaps of bales and boxes?
Such men need something to keep their hearts fresh
amidst the dragging, crushing, brain-distracting toils
that come hourly upon them; something to re-open,
from day to day, the choked up fountains of generous
sentiment; something to lift the thoughts up out of
the low and narrow circle in which they are in danger
of losing all proper freedom and vitality.

So much as this may be said even on the supposition
that the pursuits of business were to occupy a man's
chief energies to the close of life. But the time is
coming, according to the prevailing usage, when the
successful man of business will think it his privilege
to retire and turn his long-burdened mind to something less fatiguing and exhausting to his energies.
And what now is to fit him to enjoy his new circumstances? It is a lamentable fact that simply from
the want of a proper cultivation of their intellectual

faculties, multitudes of our men of business, when they come to retire to a life of leisure, do not know what to do either with themselves or the fortunes they have accumulated. They rush, perhaps, into all sorts of foolish extravagances; they make themselves and their families absolutely ridiculous by their absurd passion for show and parade; they ruin their children by the indulgence of desires which should be sternly repressed; and, after all, are restless and uncomfortable themselves, and, by their petulence or purse-proud insolence, disturb the peace and enjoyment of all within the circle of their influence. Having been mere business men during their whole active life, they now discover that they have no capacity to be anything else. Having devoted their whole souls to the mere pursuit of wealth, they find themselves utterly ignorant of its uses, and incompetent to derive from it the least real gratification.

The deplorable consequences of such neglect are often strongly manifested in their effect upon the business man's family. If he is successful, one of his first objects, generally, is to put his children into a position of honour and influence. Hence he spares no pains in their education. The best schools are resorted to. Every advantage which money could give is freely afforded them. They stand side by side with, and often surpass by their attainments, the children of the most cultivated. They are admitted into, and perhaps courted by, the most cultivated and intelligent society. And what is the result? Why, just to make them painfully ashamed of their father's ignorance. His want of culture is a perpetual mortification to them. His ridiculous blunders, his coarse and uncouth manners, his utter want of all that constitutes a gentleman, make them dread to meet him in the same company, and be responsible for his glaring deficiencies.

The attainments of which we speak are a duty which he owes to the community. By the successful pursuit of his vocation, he is brought into new and more important relations to his fellow-men. He has persons, more or less numerous, in his employ, or dependent upon his patronage. He comes in contact, in his transactions, with individuals of a great variety of character and circumstances. Men of influence, men of education and refinement, are likely to be brought more or less intimately into connection with him. He will be called upon to take part with others in matters of public interest requiring knowledge, taste, and discernment.

Many of our most successful men of business have begun life in great obscurity, and pushed their way up into significance by the force of their own shrewdness and energy. In their new position they might exercise a large influence and wield a commanding power over society; but the difficulty is, that new position is one for which they have made no sort of preparation. Instead of anticipating it as they saw themselves from year to year rising towards it, and endeavouring to qualify themselves for its high responsibilities, they have suffered their leisure hours to run to waste, neglected the cultivation of their own minds, sought for no knowledge except what related directly to

making profitable bargains, and now they find themselves in the extremely awkward and embarrassing
position of a man appointed to some high office or
trust, for the discharge of whose duties he has neither
knowledge nor capacity. Of course, their only alternative is either to creep away into obscurity and forego
their opportunities, or, by undertaking what they are
in no condition to accomplish well, do an injury to
society, and make their own incompetence only the
more conspicuous.

There are numerous important duties which this
class of men owe to their country, which can only be
performed by men of intellectual cultivation. We
have already spoken of the intimate relations which
the pursuits of men of business bear to the civilization
of the age. The policy of nations is, and ought to be,
mainly conducted with reference to the interests which
they manage. The sinews of war and the arts and
embellishments of peace are under their direction. Of
course, there is no class of men better qualified than
they to guide the counsels of the nation, if they were
only among the most intelligent. It has often been
remarked that, in our national assemblies, we have far
too great a proportion of the legal profession, and the
business interests of the country are too feebly represented. And why is this the case? Simply because
the lawyers, as a general thing, are far better acquainted
with the condition and interests of the country, and the
methods by which its needs are to be supplied. Men
of business ought to qualify themselves in these
matters, and not leave to another profession the

entire management of affairs in which their own pursuits and interests are most immediately and vitally concerned.

They owe the attainment of this class of qualifications to the cause of humanity. They are the men to whom the world looks to endow literary institutions, to afford the means of carrying forward enterprises of charity and benevolence, and to give the impulse and the direction to wise schemes for human improvement. Our wealthy merchants are, and must be expected to be, among the greatest benefactors of their age. What princely munificence have some of them exhibited! and what an honourable and endearing name have they won by it! Astor, Crossley, Brown, Peel, Chambers, and Peabody — what noble institutions have they founded! What an impulse have they been enabled to give to all the interests of learning, morals, and religion! The noble trees which they have planted will be waving their refreshing foliage over a grateful country, and bearing fruits for the sustenance of the nation and of the world, when the names of many a successful aspirant for place and power shall have faded into irrecoverable oblivion. We do not wonder that our rich merchants wish to emulate such examples. But if they would do it successfully they must not allow their minds to be absorbed all their life long in mere money-making. They must attend carefully to their own intellectual furniture and training. Ignorance, indeed, can be munificent enough. But only intelligent munificence is likely to be of real benefit to the world.

Such attainments the man of business owes to the
Church, to the cause of true religion, and to God.
The Creator has endowed us all with faculties capable of cultivation. And by so doing he has imposed
upon us the obligation to pursue that cultivation to
the extent of our opportunities. How much more
useful, in all respects, a man of enlarged and well-
informed mind is capable of making himself—in
the religious instruction of the young, in his influence
over those with whom he associates or comes in contact, in organizing and carrying forward schemes of
benevolence, in guiding and sustaining all the enterprises and activities of the Church—compared with
one who is ignorant and narrow-minded, is too obvious
to need a moment's discussion. Hence the culture in
question assumes the character of a high Christian
duty, and cannot be neglected without bringing down
the censure which our Lord pronounced upon the
slothful servant, " Wherefore then gavest not thou my
money into the bank, and then at my coming I should
have received mine own with usury?"

We have room only to offer, in conclusion, a few
brief suggestions as to the method and practicability
of attaining to this object.

It is very desirable that a broad and solid foundation should be laid for it by a good early education.
Our youth who are looking forward to a life of business should be made to understand that no narrow
and superficial school education will fit them to act
well their part, or aspire to eminence in their chosen
employment. We do not say that a college education

is necessary for all. We do not say it is the best which could be devised for the attainment of the desired object. But we say unqualifiedly, as things now are, those who are in circumstances to avail themselves of such an education should by no means neglect it; and those who are not, should secure the best substitute which their opportunities will allow. Go to school; put yourself under thorough mental discipline; learn to think, to study, to apply yourself. It is a capital error of large numbers of our young men, that they are in so much haste to get out of school and into the counting-house. It is a capital error that they value so little the advantages of their school training while they are under it. A gentleman whom we knew took his son from school early, and transferred him to a clerk's desk. On being asked why he did so, if he thought his son had acquired learning enough, he replied dryly—"Oh no, but Henry has got as much learning as will stick." Such is the case with many. The education which is given them at school is of so little value in their esteem that it will not stick. They must learn to appreciate it. It is fundamental to all subsequent attainments. Here it is that the strong, deep, broad foundation is to be laid on which to build afterwards by study, reading, observation, and reflection.

Much of the mental culture of the man of business is to be acquired practically. If he has right mental habits he will find food for thought and lessons for his instruction in all the daily occurrences of active life. Man with all his passions and pursuits, events

with all their changes, and nature with its rich variety
of beautiful, sublime, mysterious, and glorious objects
—its operations and its laws—are ever his open book.
With only the capacity to read such lessons he might
everywhere find "tongues in trees, books in the
running brooks, sermons in stones, and good in everything." But the first requisite is to acquire that
capacity. He must have learned to observe, to reflect,
to generalize, to reason. The uninstructed rustic
hears no voice when the trees whisper, and reads no
meaning syllables when the brooks reflect to his eye
the flowers that grow upon their margins, or the sun
glances his resplendent beams upon their rippling sur-
faces. So does the illiterate young clerk or the
ignorant old trader see, in all the instructive events
that pass in living panoramas before his eyes, and
chronicle themselves in his ledger and his correspondence, only the opportunity of making good bargains,
or the disappointment of his expectations of profit.
It needs an eye trained to penetrate beyond the cold
hard surface of mere gain and loss, debt and credit, in
order to obtain instruction from these sources.

It must be owned that the ordinary duties of a
business life are not favourable to a free and well-
proportioned mental cultivation. So little leisure is
enjoyed ordinarily; so close and constant is the
attention necessary to keep all things right in an
extensive business establishment; so heavy is the
weight of care that lies upon the mind; so many dis-
tracting interests clamour all day long for its attention,
that there is little room left for reflection, and still less

for reading and study. The man who purposes to enjoy this privilege has got to contend for it. He has got to overcome serious obstacles. He has got to exercise great resolution and perseverance. And this will only be where there is a high sense of the value of the attainment, and a keen relish for the pursuit.

In order to this end the method to be pursued must be arranged as systematically as possible. One hour in a day, set sacredly apart for study, will accomplish wonders as the months and years roll along. Let it be so set apart, remembered, and kept sacred, as a kind of Sabbath of the intellectual man. Who cannot at least do so much even in the busiest period of his life? Let the employments of that hour be regulated by a well-digested and fixed plan, not to be swerved from. This year and next a course of history is to be attended to. The following year the subject of political economy, or natural science, or Christian ethics, is to employ the attention. The books are carefully selected. The thoughts and arguments which they contain are thoroughly mastered in succession. Whatever is learned is learned, and once for all. Let the plan embrace such variety as may only exercise, and not weary the faculties. Pursue it steadily, month after month, with quiet perseverance, making the knowledge you acquire the food for thought whenever your mind is not otherwise occupied, and the theme of conversation when you meet with those capable of appreciating it or likely to advance your attainments; and, though it may seem that you gain little to-day or to-morrow, the result at the year's end will not fail to reward your perseverance.

In this pursuit some things are to be guarded against. Leisure hours are very easily frittered away in reading to no profit. Let the newspapers occupy only their allotted share of attention. They are valuable helpers. But they are thieves of time too. Let the trashy stories with which the market is flooded be abjured steadily. Let some easy, entertaining, and yet well-approved book, the product of some really gifted and sound mind, lie always on your table, with your place in it accurately marked, not in the book itself, but in your own mind, to occupy you in those loose moments which even the busiest have occasionally at their command.

One suggestion we would here make with the greatest earnestness. It is true, undoubtedly, that high moral and religious culture are not absolutely indispensable to intellectual attainments. But it is equally true that there are close relations between them. There is a pertinent remark of one of the profoundest thinkers of the last generation, which both the man of business and the scholar by profession would do well to ponder : "An hour of solitude passed in sincere and earnest prayer, or the conflict with and conquest over a single passion or a subtle bosom-sin, will teach us more of thought, will more effectually awaken the faculty and form the habit of reflection, than a year's study in the schools without them." And again we have the assertion from the same high authority : " Never yet did there exist a full faith in the divine Word (by whom light as well as immortality was brought into the world) which did not expand the intellect while it purified the heart—which did not multiply the aims and objects of the understanding while it fixed and simplified those of the desires and passions." The Sabbath ought, especially, to be devoted to such studies and occupations as will advance both these objects in mutual harmony. The consecration of one undivided day in every seven to the service of religion is the best intellectual boon ever offered to the business as well as to the labouring community. Let the pulpit on whose ministrations you attend be chosen with reference to its adaptation to feed and stimulate at once your intellect and your heart. Let its instructions and persuasions be listened to, not with mental indifference, or drowsy or wandering attention, but so as to occupy your best mental strength upon the thoughts which it presents. Reproduce at least a portion of your knowledge, by that best of all methods of fixing it deeply and indelibly in the mind, the instruction of the young. The Sabbath-school and the Bible-class open one of the best facilities for intellectual improvement which the man of business could desire. Let all his religious reading (and to this class of books he ought on that day sacredly to confine himself) be chosen with reference to its intellectual as well as religious merit—its fitness to inform and expand the mind, as well as to impress the heart. And above all, let the glorious old Bible, that book of books—whose language is the true "well of English undefiled;" whose style, in all the varieties of composition contained in it, is unsurpassed and unrivalled; whose conceptions are the most grand and soul-stirring, and whose sentiments the most pure and lofty—the book of

God redolent with the fragrance of heaven on every page, be made the nucleus of all his reading, and the subject of profoundest study and most inward and prayerful reflection.

It is among the prophecies of inspiration concerning the latter day—the day of glory which the Church has ever looked forward to with longing eyes—that "many shall run to and fro, and knowledge shall increase." But the subject-matter of all true knowledge, it must be borne in mind, is God, and his works and ways. Rightly pursued and apprehended, knowledge is religion, is worship, is the communion of the soul with its Maker. Our Saviour has assured us it is our highest dignity and happiness. For "this is life eternal, that they might know thee, the only true God." So is the cultivation of the faculties to be invested with the same high dignity. "Man's chief end," declares a much venerated authority, "is to glorify God, and enjoy him for ever." And how shall we better glorify him; how shall we more enhance our capacity to enjoy him, than by cultivating and improving, to the extent of our ability, those high capacities of our manhood in which our privilege is to resemble our Creator? "Let it not be forgotten that the powers of the understanding and the intellectual graces are the precious gifts of God, and that every Christian, according to the opportunities vouchsafed to him, is bound to cultivate the one and to acquire the other; indeed, he is scarcely a Christian who wilfully neglects to do so. What says the Apostle? 'Add to your faith knowledge.'"

MEN OF BUSINESS:

THEIR HOME RESPONSIBILITIES.

---◆---

ISAAC FERRIS, D.D.

MEN OF BUSINESS:

THEIR HOME RESPONSIBILITIES.

WE Anglo-Saxons speak of the true idea of home as peculiarly our own. Whether this be true or not, we cannot well exalt too highly the value of home, nor watch too tenderly over its character and interests.

Home! it is a little world; it has its own interests, its own laws, its own difficulties and sorrows, its own blessings and joys. It is the sanctuary of the heart, where the affections are cherished in the tenderest relations—where heart is joined to heart, and love triumphs over all selfish calculations. It is the training-school of the tender plants which in after years are to yield flowers and fruits to parental care. It is the fountain whence come the streams which beautify and enliven social life.

If any man should have a home, it is the man of business. He is the true working man of the community. The mechanic has his fixed hours, and when these have run their course he may, ere the day closes, dismiss all anxiety as his labour ends, and seek the home circle. Comparatively little has been the tax on his mind, and not much more on his physical system, as he learns to take all easy. But the man of business is under a constant pressure. His is not a ten-hour system, with an interval of rest; but he is driven onward and onward, early and late, without the calculation of hours. He must be employed. In the earnestness of competition—in the complexity of modern modes of business—in the fluctuations which frequently occur—in the solicitous dependence on the fidelity and integrity of others—he has no leisure moments during the day. With a mind incessantly under exciting engagements, and a body without its appropriate nutriment, he may well pant for home, and hail the moment when he may escape from his toils to seek its quiet, and its affection and confidence.

The man of business should have a home, not a *mere dormitory.* Alas! what an abuse it is to call the mere lodging-place, which a man reaches after dark, and which he leaves after a breakfast taken often by candle-light, a home. Mr. X. L. M. has a superb property, eight miles from town, on the main thorough-fare out of the city; every passer-by admires it. But what is it to him, as he scarcely sees it by daylight, except on Sunday? To what does all this outlay in garden statuary, beautiful flowers, and picturesque rivulets, amount in his case? It is his own, it is true; this gives him a feeling of independence; but what delight does he drink in, and what participation has he with his family in that which should be a common source of enjoyment? To them there is little of real enjoyment, as the feeling of loneliness mars all; while he is very much as the man who puts up for the night at the house opposite, called "The Traveller's Home." They both tarry for a night.

It is a very grave question whether a man in all this is doing himself justice, either mentally or physically—whether he is meeting, or is in a condition to meet, the claims which the members of his family have on him; and, especially, whether he thus meets or can meet his responsibility to God, who places the solitary in families; or to society, which must receive its controlling influences from his and similar circles. It is to be feared that we are degenerating in our ideas of home, as we are growing in wealth and multiplying our luxuries—that just so far as we depart from the view of home which our fathers cherished, so are we removing from our true interest, and throwing ourselves on what is superficial and ephemeral.

There are views to be taken of this important subject which lead directly to a very different course from that now pursued, and which, while they raise our estimate of home, show that great duties are involved, and that our happiness is identified with their discharge.

It is proposed to trace some of these under the general designation of *the business man at home.*

What is the business man's relation to home?

He is its Governor; he is its Provider; he is its Educator; he is its Priest.

THE HOME GOVERNOR.

The business man—the head of influence, the controlling, regulating power of the home circle—first claims our attention.

It was said of a family of peculiar idiosyncratic character, where waywardness and self-will had sway, "Oh! they came up; they were not brought up." How much of cutting rebuke was expressed in those words, and what a key it furnished to the errant courses of those it characterized! This remark tells in brief the tale of many a family circle, and at once develops the source of many evils we deplore.

Government is a divine principle, and we are so constituted that it cannot be dispensed with. It must be found wherever living creatures are found. It is the grand preservative against confusion, disorder, and the domination of evil passion. Let the reins be thrown on the neck of the young steed, and what unhappy consequences will follow! Let infirm childhood and youth have its way, and sadder still will be the issues. On this point we have much to be thankful for. In our land, domestic government and control have not been sacrificed to mere theories on the development of juvenile manliness and independence. The junior members of a family know and keep their place, and are submissive to a legitimate and necessary authority in the hands of the parent.

It is said by experienced teachers that they can tell, ordinarily, what is the influence and what the checks at home; and that there is a great want of home government, as indicated by the views and feelings shown by their pupils. In America, children are very early led to feel that everything must be subservient to their wishes—that no labour must be imposed, even in preparation for life, which would be irksome, and that the checks must be silken and soft.

What would the gardener say to the policy of suffering his plants to grow as they will, with no trimming, no training, no weeding—all luxuriance, wildness, entanglement, confusion? What hope would he feel warranted in cherishing concerning the flowering and the fruitage? But in the case of children there is something beyond mere luxuriance—there is a nature whose tendencies are to evil; and unchecked, ungoverned, they are developed in various grades of depravity, and must end in ruin if a gracious Providence does not interfere.

There must be government, and that in the hands of the father. " God hath set him to be the head of his house," and holds him responsible. For this there is no just substitution. A mother has a most important place, and her hand must be felt always; but she should not be left alone. The burden is not primarily or justly hers. Invaluable, blessed, thrice blessed auxiliary, she leads and moulds, while the authority which has chief control is one step beyond. It is unkind to constrain her to go beyond this. If called by bereaving providences to unite both in one, she has been found adequate. If maternal influence must be regarded as secondary, where authority is concerned, with all the nearness and affection involved in her relations, then, certainly, the judgment must go against the transfer to those who sustain the position of an employed governorship. It remains to be shown that a father may give to tutors and governesses the exclusive direction and control of his sons and daughters. Imperative necessity may sometimes force this upon a man, and then his circumstances exculpate him in the sight of God ; but he is not allowed by the divine constitution of the domestic circle, from mere fashion, or unwillingness to bear the trouble of it, to put off on another what belongs to himself. The violation of the law here will be as certainly followed by its appropriate penalty as in other cases. If a man's numerous engagements prevent a fulfilment of this duty he has something to reform. He has no right to entangle himself so as to be thrust out of his proper course. Here are primary, vital duties, and they should give a shaping to other outdoor matters, and not take it from them. A man may say he has not time, but if he has the right spirit he will find time. If he must be more with his children, he can and he will curtail or so modify other demands, as to be with them. The want of time, so much pleaded, perhaps in more cases than it would be pleasant to confess, grows out of a morbid appetite for business and gain. Is it not true that multitudes plunge into multiplied and oppressive engagements simply because they are in haste to be rich, and cannot wait the prudent and slower process of their fathers ?

If the business man must be the governor over his own home, the next inquiry is, What should be the character of his administration ?

A ready answer can be given. It should be distinguished by the spirit of kindness and love, mingling with authority. Some seem to think that a stern,

cold, formal, authoritative manner becomes the father
—that his dignity and influence may be lessened in
proportion as he unbends to his children. Such a
course has its influence; but it is far from desirable—
indeed positively hurtful. It tends to chill the young
heart, and keep at a cold distance, and induce rather a
feeling of fear and dread than of respect or regard.
It is much to be deplored that any man should so use
his position as to make his absence a grateful relief,
and his returning step and voice watched with a feeling of trepidation. Such a man can never expect the
young heart to bring its troubles to him for his counsel and his sympathy; but it will seek beyond his own
circle for what it needs, making friends of the sym-
pathizing without, and committing itself to auspices
which may lead astray. Such a man, with austere
manner and positive, absolute, master-like voice,
throws away the admirable advantages his position
and relation offer to carry his children with him in
the path they go. If he claim to be a good man, with
such a manner, he will induce the feeling of delight in
the bosoms of his children to get into scenes where
they may throw off restraint, and indulge feelings
which have been only dammed up by necessity, but
never directed or modified.

The period of childhood is that of warm, impulsive
feeling—of confiding love—of ready imitation of what
it loves. He who would manage his charge wisely and
successfully must not place the authority foremost. A
ready sympathy, the allowance of full play for all the
endearing actions of a little one, the manifest influ-

ence of warm love and solicitude for its welfare, even
in small matters, will secure, from the earliest years,
that regard and reliance which will make his word, his
nod, his look effective, as character is developed. Then
government will be easy, restraints will be cheerfully
submitted to, and he will become the preferred coun-
sellor and the chosen friend, when such are most required. It does not follow from this that a man must
become indulgent, and yield to the vain wishes and
imaginary wants of his children: this would not be
true love, but weakness. Such indulgence is one extreme, while the overbearing, despotic air is the other.
When the law of love is the law of the house, home
becomes the sweet retreat it was intended to be by our
beneficent Creator. And what but this law should
prevail where the relations are so tender and the interests so momentous?

His administration should be intelligent and reasonable. A man should seek to understand what is duty
in his circumstances, and what is right, and look carefully into all his relations, and understand what
belongs to each. As he is not infallible, his decisions
may be wrong and his requirements unjust. It is
not enough, in order to make an act right, that a
father requires it, though that may claim for it filial
attention and regard. A man may make his requirements on an imperfect or wrong view; his mind may
have been biased, or the tone of his own feelings may
be affected unfavourably, and then he may act unad-
visedly, and subsequently will regret the course pursued;
and then to correct what was wrong may be beyond

his power. Home government should be eminently reasonable, not asking too much nor too little—not unduly magnifying all little things and making them subjects of rebuke, and yet not omitting such little things as obviously prepare the way for other matters of high moment.

Some deem it necessary to give a reason for everything required. This may be and is well to a certain extent; but there are many things occurring in reference to which it may be impracticable, or even unwise. A child may not be capable of understanding or appreciating it; higher interests may require that a good and sufficient reason should be assumed to influence the matter; and sometimes positive evil might result if the reason for everything be committed to a child. Where the training is right, it will in such cases satisfy the juvenile inquirer that father wishes and directs him to do a certain thing, and therefore he will do it.

His administration should be firm and uniform, and not fitful, impulsive, and excited.

One of the most unhappy things which could occur with a group of little ones would be that of having a varying, vacillating head, in whose decisions no reliance could be placed. A management which to-day approves and to-morrow disapproves an act—which to-day rebukes a trifle sharply and to-morrow passes over a serious misdemeanor without a remark—which to-day draws the check strongly and to-morrow throws the way open to any indulgence—which is rigid before company and indifferent when the circle are alone—

only tends to undermine all regard, and leaves necessarily an unhappy impression on a child's mind. It
resolves all government into parental whim, or parental
weakness, or sheer policy. It is without principle: no
desirable habit can be formed under it; and youth
emerging from its influence can have no just conception
of what they ought to be or to do.

It is not assumed here that no man may change his
mode of government at any time; for he is ever learning, and may come to see that he has fallen into some
mistakes; or he may, in new circumstances which
arise, find one regimen preferable to another; or special
cases may control his mode of action. But allowing
all this, the hand should be firm and the application
of rules steady and uniform, while corrections of modes
should not be violent or great. There is no department in life in which the character given by the dying
patriarch to Reuben, " unstable as water," is not to be
deplored. What would it be in a general, what would
it be in business itself, what in friendship, what in the
various relations of affection, what anywhere and
everywhere, but an evidence of weakness? Children
are copyists, and especially of those most nearly allied
to them ; and in copying such a character, or in other
words, nurtured to go on with no fixed, settled views
of the duties of life, and seeing daily nothing uniform
in the head of the home circle, how unfitted must they
be for the relations of mature years, and what but un-
desirable influences can society expect from them?
He that holds a firm hand, and is calm, and keeps
under impulsiveness of feeling, is a wise man. He

may be conceived of as a charioteer, guiding a spirited pair over a narrow road, dangerous for the rocks and precipices that are on both sides.

His administration at home should be unaffected by the vexations and disappointments without.

Why should they who await a father's return with sunny faces and sparkling eyes suffer for the uncomfortable things which may have overtaken one in the conflicts and vicissitudes of business? or why, if at home some dark cloud may have come over the scene, should the depression be deepened, or the sadness be increased by a brow made sullen by some act of injustice or villany in town, or by a discouraged, desponding air, because some loss has been sustained? The first is clearly unjust to those at home : for why should they be visited for what is not their fault? and the latter is unkind and unwise: for why make the sad, sadder, and why double one's own troubles and unfit one's self for the duties to be performed? It is remarked that some fathers are painfully sensitive to the natural vivacity and playfulness of their children —cross, severe, and can bear nothing when business has gone ill; and all soon learn to stand out of the way and shun the risk of some unkind word or act. How unwise for a man to put away from him the panacea for what he has suffered—the affections warm, tender, most entire, which would be a balm to his wounded spirit! Such a course almost puts a man on a par with the hard drinker, who notoriously abuses those at home on his return from his carousal, however good-natured he may be at other times. Home should be a sanctuary over whose threshold and into whose shelter such things should not be allowed.

The home administration should be impartial. The children and youth of the home circle have an equal claim for such regard, and interest, and care, as their circumstances require. Some may be infirm or sickly, or overtaken by an afflictive stroke, or be more juvenile —then particular forms of care may be called for; but a difference in fundamental regard cannot be justified. One man makes pets of his girls, another, of his boys; one, of his oldest or firstborn, another, of his namesake; one, of the children of a first wife, another, of those of a second. Now, what can be the effect of these, or any similar partialities, but to build up walls of separation between children—engender unkind feelings, where all should be union and harmony? What depressions and discouragements must be felt by the neglected or the less favoured; and, on the other hand, what liberties taken, what domination exercised, by the favoured and caressed!

The history of Jacob illustrates the evils of such partiality in most touching details, and shows how it recoils on the parent guilty of it.

How can you avoid being drawn more to a child that is kind, attentive, docile, and obedient, than to one that is restive, gives you incessant trouble, and is at every opportunity disobeying? says one. Our present comfort may be abridged by the naughty one; but that is no just reason for difference of regard, and certainly none for showing a preference. If any feelings arise inclining to one rather than another, they should be jealously watched, lest their influence prevent the proper discharge of duty towards a wayward one, who, by the very fact of his peculiarity, needs special attention and care. If a man will drive away to greater extremes the little one who taxes his patience, let him show partiality, let him forego kindness to him, and he will sow seeds of discomfort, whose product will be, to himself, a heart full of sorow and trouble. No: this a conscientious father will not do; he will find some ground of hope; he will labour more assiduously to win the erring one.

The home administration should be fully appreciative of what is right and wrong—what is well or what is ill done on the part of a child. Justice is an essential ingredient of good government. Two things are contemplated here: proper visitation for deviations and the perpetration of wrong; and, on the other hand, the reward of well-doing. Concerning the former, it may be remarked, chastisements are of many kinds. The extreme, last resort is the personal infliction of the rod; and while the juvenile nature is what it is, this must, in circumstances, be employed, if a man will not spoil his child. There is a sickly sentimentality prevalent with some on this point, perhaps the result of an excessive use of the rod in some injudicious hands, and they will have it abandoned as too horrible. But the most observant know that it is wholesome that the errant one should understand that there is one at hand, if necessity require. The use should not be frequent, else it loses its effect, or only develops the spirit of a slave—of all things to be deprecated.

But that it is to be the last resort should be the rule.
The father has a heavy hand, and should try every
other mode of correction first.　There is a wonderful
virtue often in a breakfast on dry bread, with cold
water—in the loss of the privilege of a walk, a ride,
a visit, or company; or the sending to bed before
dark; or deprivation of the gifts which the other
members of a circle enjoy, &c.　Never, never, however,
should a recreant child be shut in the dark closet, or
the cellar, if a man will not injure the nervous system
of a child for life; and never should it be punished by
being forced to commit portions of the Bible to memory.
If a man wish his child to love that precious volume,
its associations should be with all that is pleasant and
desirable.

As to the other side of the account a man should
be most careful and punctilious.　A word, even a look
and smile of approbation, have a special charm.　He
who is ready to rebuke a wrong act should be as ready
to express his gratification with what is well done.
Indeed, it should be a part of his regimen to introduce
to his family every proper thing which will tend to
make his flock happy in right doing, and raise in their
minds, to a high point, the desire to meet a father's
wishes.　It has been urged by some that it is the
business of good government to see that a people have
their holidays, regarding the occurrence of these as
grand agencies in making laborious pursuits less burdensome, and as tending to better order and better
health.　However this may be, it must be conceded
that it is an important part of a wise domestic

administration for a father to break away, from time to time, from the yoke of business, and escort his children to such recreations or exhibitions as connect profit with pleasure. In all large cities such places are abundantly at hand, while the local improvements—the large manufactories—the public institutions—the various views around our harbour, give all desirable variety.

In a word, the home government should be administered *in the fear of God.* The position which a father occupies is not that of an absolute head, but of a steward. There is One above him to whom he is accountable; and from Him should he seek his rule for every day's walk, and by it shape all his acts. One of the greatest auxiliaries in his discharge of duty will ever be found to be his cherishing and strengthening, in the hearts of his children, the conviction that he is governed, in all his requirements, by the fear, in his own heart, of Him who is above all and over all.

THE HOME PROVIDER.

If we may, in any case, deduce the will of God from his visible works, we may draw man's duty to the home circle from the physical system given him—in comparison with which that of the female is weak. His is strength of muscle, power of labour and of endurance—his all the capabilities for the wear and tear and various encounter of life : and in this we certainly may see the will of Him who makes nothing for naught, that the stronger should have the charge of the more frail. No special reasoning nor special

N

training is called for here. Men fall into it naturally, spontaneously; and its fulfilment constitutes one of the sources of their cheerfulness and enjoyment in laborious pursuit. In the analysis of the influences which nerve the brawny arm—which carry forward in disheartening circumstances—which raise above losses, and which renew the courage, how much we, shall be called to set down to the dependence of and the love for the fireside circle! How much are they in a man's thoughts—how enthroned in his affections—how constant the reference to their wishes, their expressed desires, their recurring wants! This is beautiful and right; and beautiful especially because it is in harmony with our relations and the arrangements of Heaven.

Cases of exception there are. Sometimes painful bereavements devolve on woman the double responsibility of provision and training. When God has been pleased to take away the father and husband, bravely has she been seen bearing up under exhausting toil, most disinterestedly sacrificing her own comfort and health for those dependent on her under God. The careful observer is filled often with amazement and admiration when noting what is accomplished by feeble woman, as we call her in reference to her slender form, though a heroine in fact, and owns with gratitude the delightful confirmations of the truth that God is the father of the fatherless and the God of the widow.

There are some who would force woman out of her place. Now and then one meets with a poltroon—a mean animal, who has not the spirit of man, and who thrusts his wife forward to bear unnatural burdens, he being only ready to strut in broadcloth her toils have earned, and feast on dainties for which she has sacrificed her health, and play the cockney gentleman, with his cigar in his mouth, lolling in the fashionable saloon. Such men are domestic disgraces. Others, again, have with great earnestness argued that it was woman's right to compete with man in all the pursuits and honours of life ; though few, probably, have yielded to the plea. The sentiment of Mrs. Hannah More will be esteemed as especially true. She makes Urania, the personification of wisdom, say,—

> "Let woman, then, her real good discern,
> And her true interests of Urania learn.
> As some fair violet, loveliest of the glade,
> Sheds its mild fragrance on the lonely shade,
> Withdraws its modest head from public sight,
> Nor courts the sun, nor seeks the glare of light,
> Should some rude hand profanely dare intrude,
> And bear its beauties from its native wood,
> Exposed abroad, its languid colours fly,
> Its form decays, and all its odours die:
> So woman, born to dignify retreat,
> Unknown to flourish, and unseen be great,
> To give domestic life its greatest charm,
> With softness polish, and with virtue warm,
> Fearful of fame, unwilling to be known,
> Should seek but Heaven's applauses and her own.
> Hers be the task to seek the lonely cell
> Where modest want and silent anguish dwell;
> Raise the weak head, sustain the feeble knees,
> Cheer the cold heart, and chase the dire disease.
> The splendid deeds, which only seek a name,
> Are paid their just awards in present fame;

But know, the awful, all-disclosing day,
The long arrears of secret worth shall pay;
Applauding saints shall hear, with fond regard,
And He who witnessed here shall there reward."

As Home provider, the man of business will give his primary attention to what is necessary. He will then discuss how far he shall go in the way of luxuries; but by all means should make pecuniary provision for his family, in anticipation either of losses in business or his decease.

As to what is deemed necessary for a family it is very difficult to decide. If the question referred only to bare sustenance, one might readily come to a conclusion; but it is not so limited. In our artificial social state a man would be considered unpardonable if the home supply did not have due regard to the position of the family circle, and bear a fair comparison with the usages of his neighbours. Time was when it was sufficient for a comfortable liver to have half a house, or to have one spare front room for company: now the same man must have a whole house, and the first storey must be thrown into parlours. Not very long since one servant, for general purposes, was all that was deemed necessary : now the requirement is extended to two certainly, with special aid for extra occasions, and a nurse for the little ones. It is surprising to see how, with the great increase of facilities for domestic work, still the demand is for an increasing number of servants. It is not many years since the class spoken of were only occasionally favoured with a piano: now that instrument must be set down as an indispensable requisite. The same is true of the dietetic department, of our social entertainments and modes of dressing—great changes have occurred with our so-called advancing civilization. These, with other things in proportion, make it almost impossible to say what is embraced in the necessary provision for home.

It is, perhaps, true that the question is very much affected by the locality in which one lives, or the society he keeps; and then, too, by the person who pronounces in the matter, whether a judicious, well-balanced, or an ambitious housewife, or daughters whose education is of the intellect and higher qualities, or of the extremities of hands and feet.

It was said that the business man will discuss how far he shall go in the way of *luxuries*. It is conceded that there is to be an allowance of outlay in many things which are not among the indispensables, if a fair regard to a man's pecuniary condition will permit it. No man and no family are bound to live on the stinted provision of food and raiment which a straitened condition at the outset of life sternly required. If his labour has been successful, he is entitled to the increased comforts and enjoyments which he has earned. He may gratify his taste, he may consult appearances, he may fall in with the times,—in all, to a certain extent. What shall be the limitation? Several things indicate it.

I. Whatever may do prejudice to, or put in jeopardy, the pecuniary interests of a man's creditors is beyond the outlay of propriety. The relation of a man of business to the party who gives him credit, or advances him pecuniary means, or is upon his notes, is of the most solemn character. It belongs to common morality, as well as mercantile reputation, that a man should not allow such party to suffer in the least degree, or be placed in danger by any of his acts. Reckless speculation not only is prohibited, but a nice conscience would say, all unnecessary outlay, and everything which may impair the ability honorably and fully to meet all claims. In the progress of business, much is necessarily afloat, and the results are much affected by contingencies which cannot be foreseen. Hence, it is a difficult point to decide what a man can withdraw and put by in a form which will yield nothing in the great matter of pecuniary obligation. The dictate of wisdom is to be sure to be on the safe side, which is the side of honour and integrity. The neglect of this has done much to bring reproach on business men, and to make mercantile morality a burlesque. There is often cruelty, as well as disingenuousness, in the manner in which men waste, in luxurious expenditures, what belongs to other men's wives and children, and by their consequent insolvency bring loss, and often misery, on those whom every dictate of humanity and common honesty should bind them to sustain, by securing to them their dues. Men might almost as well rob on the highway, or break open one's counting-room safe, as defraud such by a great crash, brought on by extravagance and folly. In this day of costly edifices and rich furniture, and a style of living to correspond, it takes no insignificant amount to make up the proper style of a merchant prince; and if the man has not reached a point beyond uncertainty, he may leave other people to pay for his ambitious notions. It requires but a moment's reflection to satisfy an ingenuous mind that the first step towards such an issue should be most cautiously watched and avoided ; and if any family tendencies lead adversely to such course, it will only be necessary to show how much is involved, in order to quiet a rising desire for increase of style. Wives and children have hearts, and they will respond to the well-put claim of other men's wives and children, who stand in the relation of creditors. Perhaps the want of frankness here not unfrequently leads to the persevering solicitations which at length overcome a prudent man's decisions.

II. Whatever may abstract injuriously from a man's necessary business operations is beyond the proper outlay. What has been said relates to others; now, the reference is to the man himself. Capital, and skill to use it, are among the important elements of success; and no man should abstract from the former, relying on his wits to work out of any difficulties which may arise. The ready control of capital puts within a man's reach the means of availing himself of favourable circumstances which offer, as well as of being prepared for the business fluctuations which occur. If a man of a compact, snug condition has embarked, for instance, in a property improvement, and locks up thus what may constitute a material portion of his capital, calculating on the continuance of a thrifty business, he exposes himself to whatever vicissitudes may take place. The first billow of adverse character is very likely to overwhelm him, or certainly the second shock will. The cases are not few in which, in some such way, men doing a neat and an increasing business, make inroads on what is needed to maintain their favourable position, and in a little time make wreck of everything. One can visit scarcely any of our thriving towns or cities without having his attention called to fine edifices which have passed into second hands, they who began to build having gone into dependent retirement, through such an unwise course.

III. A man's outlay for luxuries is beyond the rule of propriety when its direct tendency is to injure his children. He must not merely study what will please and gratify, but what will benefit—what will cherish all those traits of character which shall fit them for the future. Now it is not to be concealed that the outlay of many parents, in their style of living, house adornments, and the various paraphernalia, and trappings, and indulgences, is most deleterious to their children. A false taste is cherished, and what is merely incidental comes to be regarded as essential. A false standard of personal valuation is set up in the mind, and real, available, solid worth is made secondary to tinsel and mere gewgaw. The whole view taken of life will be false, as its great purpose will be that of the old Epicureans—" Let us live while we live." All personal energy, all self-helpfulness, will be sacrificed to a sickly effeminacy, which must ever be waited on. The parent must die: he may die before his children; and how does he leave them—with what controlling feelings, and desires, and aims? And with what preparation to encounter the stern realities which must come upon them? As the inheritance divided will not give each what the father used, and they cannot "begin life where the father left off," how miserable must be their condition! Happy is that man who makes his expenditure such as to secure present gratification, without enervating the character; whose liberal use of the avails of a successful business shall raise the tone of the mind, enlarge the views, and cherish aspirations after something better than mere show.

IV. When an outlay for luxuries is such as to prejudice the benefactions to important public and social interests, it is beyond the rule of propriety. Bound together as society is, and constituting, in one form or another, a combination of mutual dependencies, it is the law of our condition that we should contribute to the welfare of the whole. Now it may be in the way of taxation, on the principle that the benefited should bear their share of the burdens of society, and then it may be in the way of pecuniary donation to the necessitous, and wretched, and outcast, as they are parts of the brotherhood, and aid to them is a part of the curative process which social weal demands. Apart from the views of the duty of benevolence presented in the Word of God, it is clear that a man is doing himself a service in just so far as he is the patron of all the institutions which relieve want, instruct the ignorant, take care of the young, reclaim the erring, reform evils, cultivate and diffuse sound learning and piety through all grades of social life. The more intelligence is diffused, and principle is inculcated, and industry is cherished, and the means of self-support are placed in the way of men; the more the young are trained, are separated from baneful example, are brought under healthful influences—the more society is raised, and the more certainly are peace, good order, public security, and, by consequence, private benefit advanced. These influences or modes of operation to rectify social evils, or cut off their sources, may be called, collectively, the moral police of society, and they are efficient for good just in the degree in which they are faithfully and perseveringly pursued. They have repaid the benevolent many fold, and the reason of their not yielding greater and wider results is found in the fact of a limited use.

Reference has been made to the Word of God. Here the course of duty is made plain and very imperative: " Do good unto all men as ye have opportunity;" " Omit no opportunity of doing good;" " Be merciful;" " Feed the hungry, clothe the naked;" " Freely ye have received, freely give," are among the divine injunctions. Then the most glorious and moving of all examples, that of our blessed Lord, is employed to lead in the way of an enlarged benevolence. What thrilling, heart-moving words are those of the Apostle Paul,—" For ye know the grace of our Lord Jesus Christ, that though he was rich, yet for your sakes he became poor, that ye through his poverty might be rich."

It is necessary, then, if a man would make out a

fair claim to a sound humanity, to a Christ-like Christianity—indeed, to a sound social philosophy—to hold himself bound to act a liberal part in public, social, religious, educational, and industrial benefaction. He should charge himself with it just as decidedly, and make it a part of his plan of life, as he does the payment for any other beneficially reactive matter. The true reasoning, accordingly, is, that positive claims must take precedence of mere luxuries, and as these are such, no business man ought to allow his expenditure for luxuries to impair, certainly not to prevent, his contributions to the public good, any more than he would to prevent the payment of his taxes. The plea of inability is often heard, even when the case asking aid is most important, when that inability proceeds from a violation of this rule—so much has been vainly and unwisely lavished in luxurious expenditure that selfishness and vanity are pampered at the expense of the primary claims of benevolence and piety.

Again, an outlay for luxuries, which prevents proper investment for the future, is beyond the rule of wisdom and duty. It is a common maxim that a man should live within his income, and thus have something to lay by for the winter of life. So much uncertainty hangs over our condition here, so many events, which to us seem contingencies, dash human hopes, and then we are so liable to various disabilities, that we may well look to the future, and learn a lesson from the diminutive creatures that always prepare for stern winter. It argues no want of trust in God to do so, any more than any form of preparation for a future event does. The evil is in undue solicitude, and accumulating burdens of care—not in any fair exercise of the foresight of prudence. If a man is not governed by such a policy, it is apparent how easily in Providence he may be made to feel and bitterly regret the folly of wasting on sheer frivolities what might have made old age, or a state of continued bodily infirmity, comfortable. They who have recklessly gone on, will, in the day of necessity, find every vestige or remnant of gaudy display not only a memento but a sharp reprover of their improvidence. The mode in which a prudential investment for the winter of life may be made is well understood.

It was said that, as the Home provider, the man of business should, by all means, make provision for his family in the day of his prosperity, in anticipation either of losses in business or his decease. This is taking new ground; but it is believed to be fair, and only just, to the parties to be benefited, and not in any way injurious to any. Let the matter be looked at with care. It will be conceded that it is both desirable and important that a man should guard those who are dependent on him from adverse circumstances, so far as he can honourably, and at the earliest moment. The actual history of the mercantile community shows many painful records of unexpected depressions and disappointed hopes. How often has the sun risen in splendour, but as day has advanced, dark clouds have obscured the sky, the tempest has followed in its fury, and shipwreck and ruin have closed the scene. The fluctuations of business life are proverbial, until it has become a notable fact that so few who have carried on a large and apparently prosperous business have left anything comparatively, on their decease, as the avails of a life-long labour. Serious mistakes may have been committed; even the prudent may have been induced to embark on the sea of speculation; a dishonest partner may have involved a man in heavy losses; the gains of years may have been swept away by the too great confidence in some one of even established character; a man may have been drawn down, without any fault of his, by the fall of his neighbour, as the smaller trees, able to stand if left to themselves, are crushed by the crash of the larger under whose branches they have grown; he may have become too old to vary his modes of business as the times require, and because he cannot trim to the changing winds, is left behind, and custom seeks new channels; indeed, it would be tedious to describe the modes in which fair hopes, yes, the fairest hopes, may in the progress of years be frustrated. And in this uncertain course expenses have been increasing; the family is larger—is older; bills are necessarily greater; new relations are to receive attention, and the man himself is approximating the period when his energy is less, his hopefulness less, and he needs repose, but with the harness on is wearing out rapidly. Then how quickly is the product of more vigorous years consumed, and especially if, through a protracted decline in which he is incapacitated for labour, according to the familiar remark, "all goes out and nothing comes in." It is painful to contemplate the condition of those who are left, who, from having high hopes and having been habituated to every comfort, and probably luxury, are thrust by stern necessity into the struggle with depressed, perhaps dependent circumstances. What melancholy hours are the portion of many such; how is the small pittance which may have been saved eked out; what sighs are heard after many things which in the day of prosperity were thrown away; what melting tales are heard of the manner in which one article after another, remnants of former days, are sold at a sacrifice to furnish the requisites of life. It is often said that truth is stranger than fiction—if anywhere, it is often here. Looking forward on life, the possibility of such a lot for those nearest and dearest to him, should move a business man to do what he can to anticipate it. The question is, supposing he desires it, how shall it be accomplished? Only in perfect integrity to all to whom he is indebted. A man must be just; every claim must be provided for, otherwise his arrangement would be a fraud. It is very rare that a business man, devoted to his proper pursuits, does not reach a point when he has something, more or less, over and above all claims; that after a liberal calculation of all precarious circumstances, at that given point of time he might lay aside something with the approbation of all parties. The law defines when he may make a settlement on his wife and on his children. Let him avail himself of it. Then some have said the end is answered by an insurance on his life; this is well, and should be much more resorted to; but it is exceptionable in this point of view, the annual payment may become inconvenient—in some instances impossible—and thus the whole be put in jeopardy. So a gross amount may be paid to secure an annuity; but to make this sufficiently valuable, too large a sum must at once be taken out of one's business. The most feasible mode is to make an investment in some approved form, selected with judgment, for the exclusive benefit of named persons, and give it all the accretions of annual interest and dividends or other increase. This would be effectual, and meet almost all contingencies. And it is not an unnatural stretch of imagination to picture the time when the man who could do this in the day of his prosperity may be made comfortable by it in the day of his adversity—those dearest to him, whom he has placed beyond the reach of his own depressions, being the disbursers. By such a process how many who have gone to the grave in sorrow would have been saved from the mortification which has broken their hearts!

If a man has married a wife with a property at her command, or who has inherited it subsequently, the mode of accomplishing his provision, so far as she is concerned, is easy. If they live where the law does not make it hers absolutely, or in other words, if under the system where all hers, with her person, becomes his, common honour demands that he should release it to her, and sign off all right which circumstances may have given him. That property he has not earned, nor has it been given to him: only incidentally has he a control of it. The usage opposed to the course now suggested is barbarous, and has done more to provoke the cupidity of fortune-hunters than it has done good to the right minded. Had this been the established mode always, untold miseries would have been prevented. In numerous cases such a mode of procedure would secure all that is required, and the question of provision be easily settled. But if there be no such opportunity, the voice of painful experience calls most earnestly on every man to do for his family in his prosperity what a due regard for all his liabilities shall allow him to do honourably, in anticipation of losses or of his decease.

THE HOME EDUCATOR.

This view of the man of business, in its wide range of duties, is second to none other—bearing most directly on his own comfort and that of those under his care, and most emphatically on the well-being of society. It is due, accordingly, to himself, to the home circle, to society, to give special attention to all that is involved in it. Besides, there is everything to encourage his effort, for our nature is the most educatible. The results of faithfulness here are early seen, and they abide, and in turn become the seeds of similar fruits in succeeding relations, and thus, if good, go on blessing society interminably; for right influences never die. The relation of Home educator can never be thrown off while a man has imitating beings around him, or those in any way to be influenced by him. Indeed, he is always educating others, whether conscious of it or not, and thus, as his influence tends, is either a means of good or of evil.

Education is too frequently taken in the limited, scholastic sense, but this excludes some of its most important aspects and agencies. Properly speaking, everything which draws out the constituent elements of our nature—develops, strengthens, and trains them —is educational. The man of business may say he is not a schoolmaster; but he is nevertheless playing the part of one whenever within the family group, and he cannot prevent it. The moment he crosses the home threshold, his step, his voice, his glee or his sourness, his smile or his frown, his warm and affectionate greeting of each little one or his coldness of manner and distance, his tender interest in all troubles which may have occurred or his indifference to all, are so many lessons to every member of the group looking up to him. All hearts are drawn to him—for is he not the father? In the recognition of that relation, and the feelings drawn out by it, how natural the conclusion of the young mind, what my father does is right, and I will do like him! Does he fly into a passion; does he pronounce hasty judgments; are his condemnations unjust; are his freedoms with the characters of others injudicious; is he negligent of duty; are his indulgences unseemly,—it is most probable that his boy will do the same. Does the father smoke and drink a little, the son will reason, "My father does it, and I may do it; it never hurt my father, it will not hurt me." And so it is through all the detail of life. A growing family will not fail to be docile learners of those to whom their nature teaches them to look up. Very few realize how constant and how decided the impressions made on the minds of children, and how conduct, conversation, temper, looks, and omissions, are treasured up, and mould, and train, and educate the group, which thinks it meritorious to be the counterpart of father. Let a man watch narrowly, and he will find, more than he is aware, the likeness, nearly the fac-simile, of himself, in more respects than physical features or characteristics. What a guard should a man have over himself; what care should be exercised that his children should see and hear nothing which he would not wish repeated; and beyond this, how desirable that he should so train himself that the doing and being what he would have them to be and to do should be a second nature.

A man himself educates, and he educates by others. This is true of all the associations to which he introduces his children—of all the details of social intercourse which he deems it important to observe, and of the location of home. The whole management of home is educational. Can it be a wonder, then, that society is not more pure, more elevated, more virtuous? The solution of very much that is to be deplored in social life is simply this: the home training was sadly defective and negative, or positively evil.

In reference to the education, in the stricter sense, which a man gives his children, it is to be remarked in general, that it is often the best portion he can bestow on them. That man spoke wisely who said he would make sure to give them this inheritance, whether he could leave them any other or not. Money laid out in a careful education is an admirable investment, and should be most cheerfully made, and is bestowed on the parent's most important auxiliary. Some men speak disparagingly of education, and of the men who devote themselves to it, from sheer meanness and avarice. "I have succeeded in making money without it," says a boasting ignoramus, who cannot spell correctly the bills he sends to his customers, "and my children can do as I have done. Your teachers are mere drones." What is the truth, as verified by constant observation? The office of a teacher is one of the most important in social life, and he who is really a good teacher is the common benefactor, and deserves all honour and favour. The pecuniary compensation paid him is at best a meagre return for the toil and anxiety which are the price of his success. He who treats his claim as a charity, who defrauds him of his due, who thrusts him aside as a menial, ought to know that he is ignoring his best friend, and treating unworthily the hand which, out of the crude mass, is to form the ornaments of his house.

Several questions require an answer to him who seeks to do his duty here.

I. What shall the education given his children embrace?

II. Through and by whom shall it be given?

III. Where shall it be given?

IV. When shall it begin, and how long shall it continue?

I. What shall the education embrace? There is much of an elementary kind which is indispensable,

which in all cases is the same. The clear common
sense of the community decides about this, without any
pretence to philosophy, and it pronounces the thorough-
ness of these the basis of all subsequent progress. No
parent should allow himself to be led away by tinsel
and ornament while any deficiency exists here. Pro-
ceeding from this onward, there can be no just limit;
for in the training of our nature God has nowhere
said, Thus far shalt thou go, and no farther. If a
man's means enable him, he should give all the child
will take, with special conditions—namely, all should
be useful; everything should be in due order and
proportion ; nothing should be forced, either taking
into account the nature of a study or the quantity of
work required ; the variety should not be such as to
distract the mind ; all should be made as attractive as
possible; all should be in harmony ; and the mode
pursued should be adapted to cultivate all the faculties
—the memory as well as the judgment, the imagination and the taste as well as the understanding, the
affections as well as the mind—and not any one at the
expense of the others. And especially should the
physical system be attended to. What is all intellectual and æsthetical education worth if the body
be enfeebled and sickly? A parent should see to it
that good, wholesome air circulates in the place of
instruction, and that scholastic duty is relieved by
invigorating exercises.

When speaking of the range of education, a question
has been asked, Whether a parent should be governed
by the present direct benefit of a given study ? The

answer is, he cannot be so governed, for in the whole course of our well-arranged institutions there is nothing which does not minister to desirable mental training, and is accordingly important, though how the benefit resulting may be applied in a particular case may not be at once apparent. The work is for the future. And then, as no one can anticipate Providence, a man may find that what he pronounced against as being valueless would have been the greatest blessing to his child. What shall be done with a study, say some, for which a child has no natural adaptation? A fair and full experiment should be made to settle the fact that this is so; sometimes what may be called want of adaptation may prove mere inattention, wilful neglect, opposition, or the effect of bad associations; or all difficulty may be set down to the manner in which a child is treated, or the mode in which a subject is taught. It may be the fault of the teacher, as decidedly as it may be that of the pupil, that no fondness for a study is cherished, and no proficiency is acquired. But when the point of want of adaptation is satisfactorily settled, the answer is to be decidedly this : an eclectic course must be pursued, or certain studies must be less pressed, if not omitted. Ordinarily the entire curriculum of a well-arranged educational course may be taken (not perhaps with the same success in every branch, but with fair proficiency in all, and special in some); but in many cases it is wise and encouraging to allow a choice, under the advice of a judicious friend. It is a great waste of means and time to force upon a scholar what he or she cannot acquire. Hundreds of pounds are thrown away on musical education, when there was no natural fitness for it, and upon various branches of study under similar disability. It must be allowed that all men cannot be linguists, or mathematicians, or rhetoricians, or naturalists, or all together; with a general conception of each department, they slide into that for which their preferences have been growing stronger and stronger in a preparatory career.

II. Through and by whom shall it be given? It is true in education, as in other matters, that the lowest priced is not the cheapest; while it is not true, on the other hand, that the most costly is either the dearest or best. Some things are dear at any price. So it is among teachers; and a man may better pay to have them retire. Yet there are persons who are ever seeking low-priced tuition, and such must not be disappointed if they find it, according to the price, very poor. Among teachers are persons also who can puff loudly and put their wares very high, apparently on the principle that there are parents who have more money than brains, and who love, when they are "gulled," to have it done handsomely. The man who respects himself will avoid both extremes, and will ask a compensation according to the work done. So the parent should select, as the agent to whom he commits his child, the man of integrity, who is just to himself and to his patron.

A large convention of practical men, a few years since, gave it as their opinion that lady teachers were preferable for boys up to nine or ten years old, and even older. The grounds on which such a policy would be based would be these: that that period is one which calls for sympathy, for tenderness; that it is one in which the heart must be especially cultivated; and, particularly, because the influence of a cultivated lady teacher would keep down the asperities and rudeness which under other treatment would pass unnoticed. A proper direction given under such influences is likely to be felt through life. And no scholarship is sacrificed under it; for well-taught females, as gifted as the other sex, can be obtained.

No man should entrust his children to a person deficient in principle, or given to a single bad habit. The drinker, the profane, the vulgar, the frivolous, the gambler, the dishonest, the irreligious, should in no case be entrusted with the charge of the hopes of a family. What can a parent expect from such? And even if the book instruction be sound, what will be the effect of the example? and what estimate of character will be implied, on the part of the parent, in their employment?

As children and youth are passing through the most infirm period of life, when the judgment is imperfectly developed, they should only be placed in the hands of teachers of decided heart and great patience. The place of youthful training is not the one for the petulant, peevish, passionate, the frivolous or stoical temperament. There will, of course, be much to try one, and sometimes very aggravated cases may call for treatment; yet these will not justify the ebullitions of passion against which frequent complaints are made. If there be any position in which a man should cultivate control over his own spirit, it is that of the teacher. He who has it not loses the respect of those under his care, and they will despise him, or fear him as a tyrant; and the advantages derived from any eminence of talents he may possess will be more than overbalanced by the unhappy exhibition of his passions.

Aptness to teach should be sought as an indispensable quality. It is not mere learning which constitutes a proper trainer of the young mind. A man may have vast stores laid up in the intellectual repository, and if he has not the faculty of communicating, he is comparatively useless. A parent who seeks the best interests of his children should aim to secure those who, though they may have less shining attainments, understand how to interest youth, and impart in an intelligible manner what they have acquired.

To a certain extent the teacher is the father: he personates him; is, as the technical phrase is, *in loco parentis*. In the settlement of the question, Who shall represent him? a father will then certainly insist on having a conscientious teacher—one whose high sense of honour, whose feeling of deep responsibility, will induce him to identify himself fully with parental wishes and plans, and merge self in their accomplishment—to whom it will be a matter of greater delight to secure the best advancement of his charge than any individual results which may accrue to himself. A conscientious teacher will draw his standard of duty

from the Word of God, which, while he commends it
to his pupils, he will seek to follow himself, and will
feel that his accountability is to God, as well as to him
who honours him with the training of the objects of
his dearest affections. Only such are worthy the
teacher's place.

III. Where shall the education be given? It has
become quite a fashion of late to send children away
from home for education. What are we to think of
this practice is the question? That there are cases
where this should be done, and would be best to be
done, is not to be doubted; and where such necessity
exists it will be regarded by the sensitive parent with
regret. The inability to obtain suitable advantages
near home may be a cause. The loss of the female
head of a group of children, and the unfavourable
position of the remaining parent, does often lead to it.
An infirm state of health at home may make a transfer
to a more salubrious atmosphere desirable; and other
circumstances, not specially complimentary to family
management, can be readily conceived, in which the
obvious propriety of the measure meets all inquiries.
But without some special controlling consideration,
which will justify it to his own conscience, no man
should pursue such a policy, and do the violence which
the young heart suffers on separation from home. In
the first place, he has no right to transfer his responsibilities to other hands without a sufficient reason.
God holds him directly amenable. His duty is
primary, and it is of such a nature that no one else

can really perform it. And then the risks he runs are
of the most serious character. Among these are the
loss of a home feeling on the part of his child; the
diminution of interest in his own heart; the sacrifice
of all the enjoyment connected with having his flock
around, and watching their progress and cheering
them on; the casting of his child into a circle of
influences which he cannot control, and a training in
sly trickery and selfish indulgences, which have been
complained of in the most carefully managed boarding-
schools, and which have only come to light when the
evil was done;—in a word, thrusting a child almost
entirely on mercenary services.

Some men use glowing terms in depicting the disadvantage of training boys in a city; and one would
suppose the city-bred boy must of necessity be ruined.
But it is mere talk—a cover, in many cases, for a
fashion which the parental heart should shrink from.
The truth is, there are evil influences everywhere; in
various situations various forms of evil, and all tend to
the downward road; but who better adapted to ferret
out the danger than a father? and where can a child be
safer than under a father's eye daily? It may be confidently said, that if proper care is taken, the safest
place for boys is in the home circle, where the ten
thousand nameless but felt forms of good influence are
brought to bear, and will operate now to check and
then to cheer, and constitute a lever of incalculable
power. How much of the practice spoken of may be
set down to mere selfish desire to get rid of care, and to
secure more uninterrupted opportunity for the slavery

to money-making, we do not say. Men complain of want of time to give proper attention to the oversight necessary; but where is their warrant for neglecting one of their most important duties? That excuse, want of time, is equivalent to a confession that something is wrong. If a man must have relief, why not seek it by some auxiliary in his business, and not in sending off his children? Is it true that his money affairs are nearer his heart than his care for those whom God has given him?

Again, say some, it is not good to have children grow up in so much society as we have, and amid such distractions. The simple reply is, have less. Will you indulge in the giddy round of social indulgence without calculating the cost, in the necessary results to the home group? Still others say, it is better to send children from home to learn the way of the world, and to cultivate their own resources, and not follow a parent's leading. What! is there not enough of the world before their eyes, passing to and fro daily? and as for resources, had they not better get them before they rely on them? Do we send a frail bark on the ocean without pilot and ballast? Shall a man send his sons abroad ere their principles and character are formed? Let it not be supposed, while this argument tends to keep children at home for education, that therefore the boarding-school system, as such, is undervalued. By no means; it has an important place, and that has been in the outset noted; it is only the abuse in the case against which a voice is raised. One must have little acquaintance with it who does not know cases where the boarding-school training has been crowned with the richest blessings ; still, it must be said, the domestic has a more blessed power ; and we think it must have, because it is the original, divine plan, for which the other occupies the place of a partial substitute.

Happy man he who places first among the objects of domestic interest the proper cultivation of the minds and hearts of his children, keeps them around him, observes the progress of each, cherishing with warm affection every stage of onward struggle, drinks in delight as, when the shackles of business are thrown off, he notes the work of the day and the earnest preparation for the morrow ; watches all the associations formed, and encourages what is in harmony with his own aims, and has the pleasing consciousness as he lays his own head on his pillow, that each member of his house is in his and her place of repose, safe from evil.

IV. When shall the education begin, and how long shall it be continued ? In the proper sense of training, never too early ; in the scholastic sense, not by any means as early as is the common practice. It is a cruelty practised on a little one to sit it down to book-labour at four and five years of age—shut it up in a school-room for four and even six hours per day, and restrain its little limbs in a fixed position, and the body in a stiff perpendicular posture, with all the horrors of a school-dame's anger *in terrorem* over it. It is absurd; it is unnecessary. Common sense says, let it run ; nature says, let it run; common humanity says, let it run. The ambition to show off the book attainments of a little one, at the expense of its health, is disreputable. The early years belong to the physical system, to air, to exercise. And nothing is lost; for nature, everything around, is teaching through the eye and the ear. It is object teaching, the true basis of sound and healthy progress. It is this which awakens the mind, and at the proper time will make the acquisition of the contents of books to be eagerly sought after. Whatever may be communicated in an amusing way may be done; but the first consideration is health.

Having well begun, the completion of education, if the phrase may be suffered, should not be hastened· It is a great mistake to limit the preparatory course to a fixed age, as many do. A most deplorable thing it is that children must be turned out finished men and women, as we turn out the various articles of house· hold furniture, by a short, patent process, as if mind, and character, and intelligence may be done to order. Everything is in a hurry among us, and the results savour of the forcing process.

It is painful to see the eagerness of parents to hurry the uninformed mind into society and business, at the most critical point of character, and when in a state to make the most desirable improvement. In a commercial community our business men commit a capital mistake by their policy of abbreviating the course of instruction, and inflating the minds of their sons with the notion of rushing into money-making, and realizing early fortunes. It is simply untrue that a com-

plete education is of no use to a man of business.
Through every step of an important business he must
have enlarged views, or he must fee the intellect that
has them.   And when his money is made, what is it
to him if he has not intellectual resources to fall back
on, or cultivation to enjoy it?   The confessions and
regrets of not a few retired men, their ennui, their
premature senility, tell most painfully of the want of a
culture which early education only could give.   Much
might be said here, to meet the tendencies to break off
an education at its most important stage, for the
pursuits of the shop and the counting-room, and much
to show that after his course is accomplished, a lad is
not unfitted for the details of business.   Facts in
abundance show that if there be frippery wastefulness,
expensive habits, mad and ruinous speculation, they
will be mostly found among men whose minds have
not enjoyed the benefit of a sound education.   Every
successful man of business owes it to the future of his
children, and the character of his class, to lay his
plans for as extensive an education as his opportunities
will allow.

The Priest of the Home Circle.

The man of business the priest of the Home circle!
Yes: and let not any startle at this combination.   Let
him hear Paul : "Diligent in business, fervent in
spirit, serving the Lord."   This is the most important,
the most honourable, the most blessed of his relations.
The term priest is here used in the sense of a leader,
or guide, or teacher in religion.   Before an official

priesthood was instituted, the father was the priest, ministered in holy things, and performed the sacrificial services—and since an office has been perpetuated for instruction in what pertains to eternal life, the father is not and cannot be exonerated from what falls naturally within his province. To him comes home the charge to bring up his flock in the nurture and admonition of the Lord. Fidelity here is beyond any governing ability he may possess—any temporal provision he may make—any education he may secure. It has to do with the interests of his children in two worlds, to the latter of which the present is less than a moment to a lifetime. The duty here is inalienable. He may have auxiliary agencies, and he is blessed with them, in the form of an ample juvenile religious literature—in the form of the Sabbath-school and Bible-class teacher, and especially in the person of a pious wife, the godly mother of his children; but still, the special, direct duty is his, and he may not, as he values the interests committed to him—as he values his own peace of mind, allow business to interfere with it. It can be no satisfaction to him, yes, it can only be a subject of bitter reflection to his last moment, if his children have grown up irreligious, worldly-minded, reckless of eternal things, and have so gone from his circle upon the broad area of the world beyond, through his neglect and failure to do his duty; through his allowing the business of the world to shut his eyes and his heart against their best interests.

Is the inquiry made, What shall he do for them? The proper answer is at hand.

I. Set them an example of personal regard for religion, and all that pertains properly to it. This, presented daily before them, will make an appeal which will tend, more than arguments, to fix attention and captivate the heart, and especially may this be hoped in the case of boys. This example should be comprehensive. The habitual reading of the Bible, the careful observance of the holy day of God (not making it a day of feasting, of pleasure-walking, visiting, correspondence, overlooking old accounts, or general reading), the faithful attendance on the house of God, the pure conversation, the living a life of integrity, all of which speak directly to the heart, should characterize it.

II. The faithful observance of family worship has a blessed influence in leading the young heart aright while it is to be commended, as it is in itself an important duty. It is marked in the Sacred Word as a melancholy thing to be of the families that call not on God. What more natural, more proper, than that, in anticipation of the uncertainties of the night-watches, the parent should commend the family circle to the care of Him who never slumbers nor sleeps ; and when the morning comes, that grateful returns should go up to the Divine Shepherd, and that in all the exposures of the day his care should be sought ? In the habitual observance of such service the young heart has brought before it, in touching form, its dependence and its obligations, and the thoughts and general views and conduct of the day are most likely to be viewed in reference to God. All the exercises of such occasions should be brief, cheerful, comprehensive. No man need feel a difficulty here for want of gifts ; for there are within his reach various auxiliaries, in the form of books of family devotion, which he may use.

III. He should take his children to the house of God. To send them is one thing; to take them with him still better, and the true course. God has eminently honoured fidelity in this respect. The fact of Divine institution, regard for his children, respect for the minister, the influence on society, as well as desire directly for religious benefits, unite to urge it. Regularly, punctually, uniformly, and always when the sanctuary is open, should be the rule.

IV. The furnishing a carefully selected religious literature is of immense moment. Time was when this was out of the question ; but not so now. The matter of most difficulty now is selection ; but this need not leave any man at a loss. Biography, missionary research, narratives, and allegories are at hand, as well as the more direct religious exposition.

V. A man should have special regard to the associations of his children, the whole arrangement of social intercourse, and the gratification furnished to his young flock. These, if not attended to, may undo all he has done, and pervert and alienate the heart he would win.

That man of business who sustains a family relation lives under heavy responsibilities. His children have claims on him, society has claims on him—above all, God has claims on him. As the Home Governor, the Home Provider, the Home Educator, and especially as the Priest of Home, he needs to look personally for the divine aid. Favoured lot, his ! He has every encouragement to commit himself and all his to the hand which places the solitary in families. Before him opens a future full of hope. The promise is, our "labour is not in vain in the Lord." Successful in securing the object of his deep solicitude, what a circle, in advancing years, may he hope to gather around him, to cheer the decline of life; and what a glorious reunion will that be when he and they shall meet before the throne of God and the Lamb !

MEN OF BUSINESS:

RESPONSIBILITIES AS CITIZENS AND CHURCH MEMBERS.

———————◆———————

WILLIAM B. SPRAGUE, D.D.

MEN OF BUSINESS:

THEIR RESPONSIBILITIES AS CITIZENS AND CHURCH MEMBERS.

IN the largest sense of the phrase, men of business, must be included all those whose time is employed for purposes of profit or improvement—all, indeed, except such as are rendered inactive by disease or infirmity on the one hand, or inclination or habit on the other. The statesman, who watches the interests of his country with a devotion that never tires; the lawyer, who works night and day to secure a triumphant issue of his client's cause; the minister of the Gospel, who counts no sacrifice dear that may be necessary to accomplish the great ends of his office; the physician, who, in obedience to the midnight call, hurries away to the dwellings of the sick ; the schoolmaster, to whom is entrusted, in a great degree, the development and direction of the youthful mind; and the farmer, whose vocation, involving obedience to the very letter of the Divine command, stands honoured in the sight of both God and man ;—all these, I say, are, in an important sense, men of business; and each is necessary to preserve the balance, and carry forward the purposes of human society. In the present paper, however, I shall consider the phrase in a more restricted sense, as applying chiefly to those who are engaged in the different branches of commerce and the various mechanical arts, and in conducting banking establishments and other institutions connected with the financial interests of a community. I will endeavour to illustrate, briefly, the responsibility of this class in reference to civil government, the Church, and the great benevolent institutions of the age.

I. CIVIL GOVERNMENT.

Whether the legitimate blessings of which civil government is the divinely constituted medium are to be realized, or in what measure they are to be realized, depends chiefly on the character of those to whom its administration is entrusted; and that this is determined in a great degree by business men, no one who reflects at all can fail to perceive. For, in the first place, every business man, in common with the rest of the community, has a vote ; and in this point of view the numerical weight of this class is immense. But there are other considerations beside numbers that go to heighten their influence in regard to popular elections. The farmer, though he may have a well-considered opinion in regard to the comparative merits of different candidates, and may express it freely as he finds opportunity, yet, from the very nature of his occupation, he has access to comparatively few other minds, and he is satisfied for the most part with reading the newspaper reports of what is going on around him, and occasionally commenting upon them to a neighbour, without even aiming at anything in the way of direct control. The business man, on the contrary, is constantly brought in contact with others—has an opportunity of communicating his views and hearing theirs in return—of discussing the character and claims of opposing candidates, and of exerting not only a direct, but often an extensive influence to secure or prevent an election. Moreover, there is an energy imparted to the mind by business habits which makes itself felt beyond the routine of daily engagements, and especially in a matter so identified with all the great movements of society as the choice of rulers. Hence it is manifest that this class must necessarily exert a mighty power at the ballot-boxes; and they are responsible for the manner in which this power is used. Providence has given them peculiar facilities for assisting to exalt good men to places of honour and authority, and woe be to such as neglect or abuse this privilege.

But if business men have a primary influence in the election of rulers, it is for them too, chiefly, to decide the measure of co-operation that rulers shall meet, in carrying out the designs of government. Those who occupy high places, however they may be envied by the multitude below them, are really legitimate subjects for sympathy, in consideration of the manifold labours to which they are called, of the opposing interests which they have to adjust, and of the temptations by which they are often beset to make shipwreck of a good conscience. It devolves on business men, more than any other class, to determine whether they shall find the administration of government attended with greater or less difficulties; whether the great interests of the state or the nation shall be properly attended to or shall be sacrificed to the jealousies, and rivalries, and collisions incident to the malignant fever of party spirit. If this great and influential class, or any considerable portion of them, array themselves against the civil authorities in the faithful discharge of their duty, it cannot otherwise be than that the machinery of government will be retarded or rendered irregular in its movements, and not improbably some disastrous result will be worked out. There is often a diseased state of the public mind which passes under the name of a panic, which usually originates with business men, and of which they are more immediately, if not exclusively, the subjects. Such a state of things is eminently fitted to impair general confidence in the "powers that be;" and while, at least by an indirect influence, it acts injuriously upon them, it is equally certain to have a disastrous reaction upon those by whom it is excited; and thus the energies of government become sensibly impaired. Let rulers do their work as faithfully as they may, there will be occasional financial embarrassments— dark clouds obscuring the commercial horizon, which no human sagacity can anticipate and no human power prevent; and yet nothing is more common, and surely nothing more unreasonable, than for those who suffer from such a state of things to lay it to the charge of those in authority, as if they were of course responsible for whatever of evil may be inflicted by the providence of God or the villany of man during their administration. It were a dictate of justice, in such cases, to sympathize with rulers, rather than to indulge impatient and bitter complaints of them ; and even where they are justly chargeable with imprudence, not to say an absolute dereliction of principle, it were far better to wait—not, indeed, without suitable remonstrance, or, as the case may be, even expostulation, but without restless and indiscriminate abuse—for the next visit to the ballot-box to work a favourable change. Bad rulers only become more exasperated by fierce opposition; their administration gathers poison from all the hard paragraphs they read, and all the bitter words they hear, which is sure to be subsequently exhaled in acts still more oppressive ; and the best service that can be rendered to society is to tolerate them in as much quietude as may be, as long as they must remain, but to vote them intolerable the very first moment there is an opportunity.

Let it further be borne in mind that the class of which I am speaking, far more than any other, are brought in direct contact with the government; for while they look to it for the protection of their various commercial and financial interests, the government, in return, exacts from them a tribute in aid of its own operations. Here is a field in which the business man often has the opportunity (and, alas! too often improves it) to indulge his cupidity for wealth at the expense of truth, justice, and honour. He who would be as quick to recognize the obligation of dealing fairly with his fellow-man, and to resent the imputation of fraud in any private transaction, as any other, seems not unfrequently to regard the public revenue as little better than a matter of private plunder; and a cheat committed upon the custom-house officer is more likely to be recalled as an instance of shrewdness or good luck than as an outrage upon the common weal, or an offence against God. And yet, so far as the nature of the act is concerned, it matters not whether the object against which it is directed be an individual or a community; for though the evil might seem to fall more heavily upon one than upon many, yet it is by no means certain but that, in its ulterior consequences, it might act with a more malign influence, even upon individual interests, than if it had been limited to a single person in its original design. Let every business man feel, when he is tempted to defraud the public treasury by concealment, by bribery, by false representations, that if he yields he is playing the part of a traitor towards the government that is sworn to guard his rights and promote his interests; and that, however he may succeed in wearing the mask, he is really an offender against integrity and honour, against his country and his God. And it is not enough that he avoid such dishonest and dishonourable acts himself; he is bound to discourage, if possible to prevent, or, as the case may be, to expose them in others; and by every means in his power to co-operate with the government in securing to it its just dues, as well as carrying out its legitimate ends. Let this numerous and active class of citizens be scrupulously faithful to their obligations in this respect, and we should quickly find a new era of public prosperity opening upon us.

Is it not true, then, that business men have a mighty responsibility resting upon them in connection with the operations of civil government—especially a government constituted like ours, which is so immediately identified with the will of the people, and which that will may at any time modify by a change of rulers— a change in which business men have always a leading agency? Who can estimate the amount of influence which they may exert, must exert, for good or evil, at this fountain of public weal or woe? Let them remember that the action of the government is in a great measure, though indirectly, controlled by them; that it is for them to say whether its movements shall be easy or difficult; that other classes virtually implore them to be faithful to their interests as well as their own.

II. But the responsibility of this class has respect not more to the government than to the CHURCH; it is here, indeed, that their influence is most vitally felt; and it operates through channels analogous to those by which it reaches the springs of civil government.

The most obvious thought which occurs in illustration of this point is that business men have a most important part to perform in reference to the Christian ministry. The Church is indeed, in the order of nature, anterior to the ministry; but the ministry acts as an handmaid to the Church; indeed, it is the divinely appointed instrument by which the Church is to collect her members and achieve her victories. And the character of the Church at any given period may be learned with almost infallible certainty from the character of her ministry. "Like people, like priest," is descriptive of an important feature of both the Jewish and the Christian dispensations. Whether we contemplate the Church on a broad or a narrow scale; whether we note its movements for an age or for a year; whether we take in the whole body of Christ's professed followers or limit our view to one denomination, or even to the worshippers in a single sanctuary, we shall find that, with few exceptions, it takes the character which a previous knowledge of its ministry would have led us to expect. An enlightened, evangelical, discreet, and earnest ministry, on the one hand, just as naturally forms a church to an exalted type of intelligence, public spirit, and devotion; and an ignorant, conceited, worldly, or blustering ministry, on the other, just as naturally imparts to a church its own leading characteristics as any other cause produces its effect. Whatever, then, affects the ministry touches vitally the well-being of the Church. Whoever contributes in any way to elevate or to depress this divine institution in the regards of the community is, for that reason, to be reckoned a friend or a foe to the Church. A moment's reflection will show us that business men have here a responsibility which it is not easy to measure.

For here, as in respect to civil rulers, their numerical importance gives them great influence. If a minister is to be chosen, especially in a populous place, you cannot fail to be struck with the fact that a great majority of those on whom the choice devolves are business men. If the congregation are in doubt in

respect to a candidate, and wish to obtain the opinion
of some of the best judging among their own number
in regard to his qualifications, you will find that, in a
vast majority of cases, the delicate office of hearing and
deciding for the rest will be entrusted to a few business
men. And if there are other important preliminary
arrangements to be made, the same class will almost
certainly be put in requisition to make them. The
fact that their respective vocations bring them so much
in contact not only with each other, but with all other
classes, in connection with the habit of prompt activity
which almost necessarily results from their daily employment, secures to them an influence in deciding the
important question of the settlement of a minister
which is peculiar to themselves. Whenever a congregation, especially a large and important congregation,
is vacant, the magnitude of the interests involved
in the question how that vacancy shall be supplied
outruns all human comprehension. But that is the
question that business men chiefly have to settle. It
is for them to say whether there shall be a bright light
fixed in that candlestick, that shall shine by an hered-
itary influence upon many successive generations; or
whether it shall be a dim light that shall scarcely
show the path to heaven; or whether there shall be a
gloomy and protracted vacancy there, which shall be
shared by a chilling worldliness and a frenzied fanati-
cism. Surely this is a responsibility that may well
make them pause, consider, even tremble.

The minister is now chosen; and the proper ecclesiastical authorities have sanctioned the choice, invest-

ing him with the legitimate rights, and charging him
" to be faithful to the duties " that belong to the pas-
toral office. But he is made of flesh and blood, just as
other men are; he has physical wants, in common
with his neighbours, that must be supplied; he probably has, or will have, a family to be provided for;
and as he depends upon his vocation, as truly as other
men depend upon theirs, for a support, to whom but
the people he serves is he to look for the competent
provision ? This, indeed, is presumed to be definitely
arranged as a preparatory measure to his settlement;
but it sometimes happens that promises which were
made in good faith are but tardily or imperfectly
fulfilled, or that, upon change of times or circumstances, the pledged stipend proves inadequate; and in
either case pecuniary embarrassment ensues, no matter whether the world take cognizance of it, or whether
it be struggled with as a painful secret in the sufferer's
own bosom. If a man of any other profession or occupation becomes crippled in respect to his finances, he
can legitimately resort to other kinds of business to
meet the exigencies of his condition; but if a minister
do that, he does it, in all ordinary cases, at the expense
of lessening his official weight, if not of really secular-
izing his character. Many a faithful minister who has
been placed in these embarrassing circumstances has
had his heart rent by the alternative of knowing that
his honest debts must remain uncancelled, and his
family be scarcely provided with even the necessaries
of life, or else he must make some movement to
retrieve his condition that shall bring him into such

close contact with the world as both to mar his reputation and impair his usefulness in his appropriate
field. Now, it devolves upon business men especially
to consider and provide against all such painful exigencies. Let them show themselves ready to minister
to all the reasonable wants of him who ministers to
them; let them be quick to discover his needs, so
that he shall not be subjected to the mortifying necessity of seeming to take on the character of a beggar;
let them act habitually in the faith of that inspired
declaration, "The labourer is worthy of his hire;" let
him be able, through their justice—for I will not speak
here of generosity—to claim all his time for the appropriate duties of his high calling; and then it will be
his fault, and not theirs, if, in his ministrations, there
is any lack of service towards them. Happy, thrice
happy, is that minister who is cast in the midst of a
congregation whose character is a pledge that, with
reasonable prudence on his part, he has nothing to fear
in respect to worldly embarrassment; whose enterprising, enlightened, conscientious, and liberal business
men are always watching his interests with an almost
fraternal regard, and not unfrequently surprising him
with their generous benefactions.

There are other concerns belonging to the same
category with the support of the ministry, which require the thoughtful and liberal regards of business
men,—especially the building of churches and other
humbler edifices for religious worship, and purposes of
kindred interest and importance. "Time, that doth
all things else impair," after awhile leaves its finger-

prints upon our sanctuaries; and however they may be gratefully associated with the memories of our fathers, whose hands reared them, and whose devout spirits consecrated them, we are obliged, by reason of their dilapidated state, or in obedience to the taste of the times, or perhaps to accommodate a growing population, to take them down and build greater, or more beautiful, or more commodious. But this is a work of thought, and labour, and expense; there are often delicate and perplexing questions involved, which it requires great sagacity and discretion to meet; and sometimes there are opposing interests to be reconciled, that may seem to hazard the success of the project; and there is a considerable amount of pecuniary means requisite—generally much larger than is originally contemplated. Here again the demand is chiefly upon business men. Others, indeed, lend a helping hand— especially educated and professional men by their wise and judicious counsels; but it is to the mechanics, the merchants, the bankers, that we look more especially to engage actively in the project, and speed it onward to its completion. I might say, with comparatively few exceptions, that every church in the land is a monument, to a greater or less extent, of the enterprise or the munificence of business men.

And there is the Sabbath-school. Upon whom, if not upon our young men of business, are we to depend chiefly for sustaining and directing that? Here, indeed, is a noble field for the display of female beneficence; and it is an occasion for devout thankfulness that so many of the gentler sex are found more than willing to occupy it; nor can it reasonably be doubted that this circumstance constitutes one of the most important elements of the efficiency of the institution; but after all, they who have the primary agency in establishing and guiding Sunday-schools are the young men whom, during the week, you will find scattered about in warehouses and workshops, insurance offices and banks, labouring diligently in their respective callings. The habit of mental activity which they contract from the prosecution of their daily business, naturally quickens their mental operations in respect to other matters; especially are they prepared to address themselves with proportionably greater vigour and earnestness to their duties as Sunday-school teachers. And I may add, they have many opportunities, in the course of their business, to enlist the influence of others in aid of the object; to persuade children and youth who are not yet in the school, to join it; and to quicken the sense of responsibility in reference to the same subject on the part of parents. Let them bear in mind that the Sunday-school to which they belong is, by common consent, placed peculiarly in their keeping—that while others are bound to labour, as they have opportunity, for the advancement of its interests, it is for them, more than all others, to decide whether it shall become more extended and benign in its operations, or whether it shall be left to languish into a state of inefficiency that may prove the harbinger of its complete extinction.

It belongs, moreover, chiefly to this class to determine, so far as human agency is concerned, the actual state of religion in a community. As business men respect or neglect Christian institutions—as they walk in the fear and love of God, or show themselves indifferent to the divine precepts—it may confidently be expected that religion will be in a flourishing or a depressed state; and that not merely from the fact that they constitute so large a class, but from the influence which their relations to society necessarily secure to them. We may illustrate this thought under two or three particulars.

With nothing is the progress of religion more immediately and essentially connected than a regular attendance on the public services of the Sabbath. Let these be deliberately and voluntarily neglected by the mass of any community, and we have no occasion to inquire whether or not Christianity exists there in its living power; for the very statement of such a fact is but another mode of saying that if there be any true religion there, it is, at best, in a sickly condition. On the other hand, let the ordinances of Christ's house be diligently and punctually attended to, and let the surrounding population make it a matter of conscience to be in the house of God on the Sabbath as often as its doors are open to welcome them, and no higher evidence need be asked for, that there the general tone of religion is healthful and vigorous. Which side of this alternative is to be realized, I say again, it is left, in a great measure, with business men to determine. It is lamentable that too many of them find an apology for being at least irregular in their attendance at the sanctuary, on the ground that the intense occupation

of the week renders it necessary that they should spend
the Sabbath in absolute repose ; while many more, it is
to be feared, are so eager in their worldly pursuits that
they suffer them even to infringe upon holy time, and
stay away from church because they cannot spare from
their business the hour that others devote to the service
of God. And I may say in this connection, that in no
way is the Sabbath more frequently profaned by business men than in travelling, either by public or private
conveyances. Would that this charge could be sustained against those only who make no profession of
their faith in Christ, and who, therefore, are not amenable to the Church for the violation of Christ's commandments; but the melancholy fact is that many
whose presence is always expected at the communion
table, and some even whose general character would
seem inconsistent with such a delinquency, are still
occasionally found on railways and steamboats during
the hours of the Sabbath, with no better apology than
that they are away from their families, and wish to
lose no time in returning to them. I will only say
that professors of religion who do this assume a responsibility which they can very ill afford to bear.
They venture in the face of the world to violate one of
the plainest of God's commandments. How they can
do this and keep a conscience void of offence—how they
can do this and not feel that they are chargeable before
God and man with the grossest inconsistency—is a
problem which must be left to them to solve.

Whether or not the occasional services that are held
in the church during the week are to be well or ill

sustained we must also look to business men to decide. These services are not, indeed, strictly of divine institution, and therefore we have no right to exalt them into the same category with the services of the Sabbath, or to make the observance or non-observance of them a test of Christian character; but that they are, when properly regulated and not unduly multiplied, an important auxiliary to Christian growth, and a fitting antidote to a spirit of worldliness, none, it is presumed, who have had experience will hesitate to affirm. Will business men encourage by their presence, and as the case may be, their more positive aid, this noiseless but efficient instrumentality for the promotion of the Church's spiritual prosperity? Will they endeavour so to adjust their secular concerns during the week as to leave time for the weekly lecture or the weekly prayer-meeting, so that this shall form a part of their regular routine of duty? Will they even give to these religious duties the precedence of secular engagements when the latter press with more than common urgency; thus at once giving evidence of their spirituality and their desire to increase it? Or will they in their conduct ignore the very existence of these religious exercises? and shall the year open and close upon them without their having so much as once joined in these weekly devotions of their brethren, or heard these more private teachings of their pastor? It is for them to decide whether they will adopt the one course or the other; but as they decide, it is not too much to expect that the tone of religious character around them will be elevated or depressed; and possibly their course may involve the determination, so far as it rests with man to determine, whether the Spirit shall come down like the rain from heaven, or whether the surrounding community shall be, in a spiritual sense, as a dry and thirsty land where no water is.

Let the business men of a church show themselves faithful to all their Christian obligations; let them not only attend regularly and devoutly upon all the means of grace, but keep their hearts with all diligence, and resist the first inroads of a worldly spirit amidst the cares and temptations incident to their daily occupations; let them, in a word, show themselves decided and earnest Christians; and they can have no adequate conception of the amount of good which they will thereby accomplish. That they are placed in circumstances involving powerful temptations to the neglect of the more spiritual duties of the Christian life, and sometimes rendering these duties a matter of great difficulty, cannot be denied; but these very adverse circumstances, by being resolutely and successfully met, impart fresh vigour to the spiritual system, just as the physical powers are braced and strengthened by exposure and toil. If you will look for the individual who has come nearest to the stature of a perfect person in Christ, you will be most likely to find him among those who have had to encounter the greatest difficulties in their spiritual course; and you will find that his attainments are to be referred in no small degree to that watchful care, that vigorous effort, that unyielding resolution, that has been necessary to save him from falling under the influence of temptation.

If we observe how large a proportion of the members of the Church consist of business men, we cannot fail to see that they must have much to do in determining the general tone of religious feeling and action. Let them be watchful and earnest Christians, and the church to which they belong will give out no feeble or dubious light. She will be an epistle for Christ, known and read of all men. But these men, being thus conformed to a high standard of Christian character, will not live for themselves alone,—they will exert a mighty influence upon the surrounding world. Let it appear that their religion is an all-pervading principle—that they are Christians in the week as well as on the Sabbath—that, while they reverence God's institutions, and delight in exercises of devotion, they never stoop to a dishonest or dishonourable, or even doubtful action, in the prosecution of their worldly business; let them, I say, thus let their light shine, and I hazard nothing in saying that the world will not only take knowledge of them that they have been with Jesus, but will feel the quickening power of their good example. The multitude with whom they are brought in contact from day to day, and who witness their integrity, and humility, and devotion, and especially their conscientious adherence to principle while they are acted upon by temptations that sweep others away, will not be able to resist the conviction that their religion is a living reality; and there is good reason to hope that some of them at least may open their own hearts to its renovating power.

Blessed be God ! Christianity has always had its full share of witnesses in the ranks of men of business ! I might refer to many noble examples of this now among the living—men distinguished alike in the walks of busy life and in the walks of Christian life; but I will limit myself here to a single case, and that shall be taken from among those who have already passed to their reward.   I refer to the illustrious JOHN THORN-TON.   As a business man he was at the head of the mercantile community in London.   He had a hand in all the great commercial movements of the day. Probably there was not a merchant then living who, in point of careful attention, of honourable enterprise, of splendid success, could be regarded his superior; and yet it would have been difficult to find among his contemporaries one whose heart beat more warmly for the interests of Christ's kingdom, or whose hand moved more freely to sustain and advance them, or whose life was more emphatically a life of faith on the Son of God.   He not only showed the practicability of uniting the eminent merchant and the eminent Christian, but he left behind him a savour of piety that will last as long as the world stands.   Not every merchant, indeed, if he does his best, can become a Thornton; but every one may be an active and devout Christian, and may learn from the record of Thornton's life how to unite commercial and religious activity.

III. But I am to consider the responsibility of busi-

ness men in yet another aspect,—I mean in its relation
to THE GREAT BENEVOLENT INSTITUTIONS OF THE AGE.
These institutions may naturally enough be divided
into two classes: those which are more immediately
concerned in the propagation of the Gospel, and which
are designed to act directly upon men's spiritual and
immortal interests, and those which look more to the
interests of the life that now is—that have respect to
the intellectual, social, and civil condition of the world.
And there are some that are of a mixed character,
having regard to both the present and the future—to
man's welfare as the creature of a day, and to the
higher interests of the world to come.   Indeed, this is
true to a certain extent of all truly benevolent institutions ; for man's entire existence is a unit—his entire
nature is a unit ; and whatever is adapted to subserve
any of his true interests has an indirect bearing upon
all of them.

In the first of these classes may be included all
Missionary, and Bible, and Tract societies, and other
kindred institutions, which, during the last half century particularly, have been multiplying so rapidly in
various parts of Protestant Christendom, and making
such a vigorous onset upon the territories of darkness.
To the second class belong all our industrial and
economical associations—all that are designed to aid
the interests of agriculture, commerce, or manufactures
—all that contemplate the progress of the human
intellect, the advancement of civilization, the perfection of civil government, or the mitigation and ultimate removal of any of the great evils incident to

human society. In respect to both these classes, as well as any that are of an intermediate character, it may safely be said that the burden of responsibility rests upon business men.

If we trace these institutions back to their *origin* we shall find that but for the agency of this class of our citizens, most of them, to say the least, would never have had an existence. Be it so that those associations that are more strictly of a religious character have been more commonly suggested and projected by ministers of the Gospel, yet in almost every case they have had some of the more active and enterprising spirits in the community associated with them; and the latter have generally had quite as much to do as the former in so arranging things at the outset as to promise a successful result. The skill and tact which they have acquired in connection with their business habits have availed them much in framing and putting in motion systems of moral machinery designed to operate for the renovation of the world; and they have not unfrequently discovered in a projected plan serious errors that needed to be corrected, or weak points that required to be strengthened, which no other than a practised eye like their own could detect. But in regard to those institutions which are of a more general and secular character, it is not too much to say that they originate almost entirely with men of business. The different professions may indeed be represented at their organization, and may sometimes bear a very important part in it; but if you inquire for those who have done the most,

you will find that they are the men who have left
their stores and warehouses to come and labour thus
for the public welfare.

If we inquire further on whom devolves the
responsibility of sustaining our benevolent institutions,
we can reach no other conclusion than that it is upon
our business men. Facts prove abundantly that it is
so, and a moment's reflection will show us why it
must be so.   For, in the first place, these are the men
who generally have at their command the means of
sustaining these institutions.   It is with this class that
much the larger part of the wealth of the entire community is lodged. Not a small portion of them,
indeed, have begun life with nothing; but by industry,
economy, perseverance, they have come in possession of
a large estate, and every year and every month is adding largely to it.   And even those who are less prospered are commonly able to secure such a competence
as will justify them in the indulgence of a benevolent
spirit towards at least some of the great objects which
solicit their aid.   But while these are the men who
have generally the means to bestow, they are those
also who, from their peculiar circumstances, are most
likely to be willing to bestow them.   There are,
indeed, some rich men who have retired from business,
and, I may add, some who were never engaged in
active business, who evince a noble spirit of liberality,
and keep themselves almost as busy as the busiest in
dispensing the bounties which Providence has entrusted
to them.   But it must be acknowledged that these are
exceptions from the general rule.   It much more fre-

quently happens that if you approach the man who
has retired upon a large estate, with an application for
charity, you will find him with his hand clenched
against the claims of your object, or if he opens it at
all, it will be sparingly, and grudgingly, and to little
purpose. Such a man, no matter how large his regular
income may be, feels that his machinery for making
money has stopped, and that naturally makes his
benevolent pulsations more sluggish; whereas, on the
other hand, the man who is still actively and prosper-
ously engaged in worldly concerns can give away even
profusely, and yet take but little note of it, because he
confidently expects that *what* he gives will quickly be
made up to him in the ordinary routine of his business
engagements. I have my eye upon a man at this
moment whose unceasing activity in his worldly calling is not exceeded by that of any other man I know,
and yet whoever approaches him for pecuniary aid—
whether it be the beggar for money to pay for his night's
lodging, or the agent for some great scheme of public
beneficence asking for thousands—his heart and hand
are always open, and his very countenance shows that
it is no self-denial to him to be charitable. I can
think of another man who used, when he was at the
head of a great commercial establishment, to be accounted liberal—at any rate, I know that many individuals and several institutions were the better for his
benefactions: but having made his fortune, he has
retired to enjoy it; his mind and body have together
become inactive; his hand will now scarcely open even
to the imploring voice of suffering; in short, he has

sunk into the indolent and sensual enjoyment of himself. This latter may indeed be an extreme case; but
it is a fair representation of a large class of cases, so far
as respects the chilling influence of the change from an
active to an inactive life upon public spirit or Christian
beneficence.

And here I cannot but drop a word in the way of
protest against the practice which has never been uncommon, and which certainly is not now upon the
wane, of men who have been largely engaged in commercial or other business, when they have reached a
certain point, settling down into a state of inactivity
in order to enjoy their fortunes. I do not mean that
it is not perfectly proper that men who have for many
years led a busy life, and been much engrossed by
worldly care, should in process of time relax from
their severe labours, and even avail themselves of the
facilities for comparative repose which their successful
enterprise may have secured to them. Still less do I
mean to intimate that they are bound always to continue in the same vocation; or that they may not
even, in the technical sense of the phrase, "retire
from business," and still have an abundance of useful
occupation. What I would bear testimony against is
a deliberate settling down in the midst of a profusion
of this world's bounties with nothing to do. The
evils connected with this are manifold. The man
who has been active for half a century cannot, if his
various faculties are spared to him, form a habit of
inactivity then without making himself wretched.
The mind that has so long been kept bright cannot be

left to rust, the hands that have so long been kept busy cannot be habitually idle, but that the curse that always hangs upon the footsteps of indolence will quickly begin to develop itself. Presently you may expect that a morose and impatient spirit will imprint itself upon the countenance and breathe through the lips; and at no distant period you need not marvel if the man who went into retirement to enjoy his fortune should be found taking on the character of a misanthrope or a hermit. And then let it not be forgotten that this man has resting upon him obligations to society, obligations to the Church, obligations to God, as truly as when his faculties were kept in vigorous exercise; and what sort of material for his final reckoning is that which he is accumulating by this habit of indolent, selfish, I may say brutish indulgence?

It is to be reckoned among the propitious signs of the times that the spirit of Christian liberality and public enterprise is constantly assuming a more vigorous tone, and promises to become ultimately the reigning spirit of the business community. Who are they who, when our great missionary institutions are ready to falter in their operations, if not absolutely to stand still, are most ready to step forward, and by their subscriptions of hundreds and thousands to put the machinery at work again even more vigorously and effectively than ever? They are our business men. Who are they who are most ready to sustain hospitals for the sick and almshouses for the poor, and to make the prisoner's life a process of reform,

and to carry into his cell as many comforts as may
consist with the legitimate operation of the penal
sentence? They are our business men. Who are
they that sustain the great interests of education and
public improvement—that plant colleges and endow
professorships, and build observatories by which heaven
and earth are brought into new relations with each
other? Here again I answer they are our business
men. There are on every side of us princes in liberality as well as in wealth; men to whom the mere
presentation of any object of public importance is a
sufficient pledge that it shall be provided for; men
who greatly lighten the burden of solicitation by
keeping an eye out and a hand open for every great
exigency; and there is everything to indicate that
these mighty men in the walks of beneficence will
increase until the world shall brighten into a great
field of millennial glory.   .

I may be allowed to remark in this connection that
there is probably nothing that interferes more with
a due regard to objects of benevolence on the part of
men of business than the mistaken idea that the interests of their children will be promoted by their being
left rich. It is wonderful how much the sagacity of
men who are acknowledged to be shrewd on all other
subjects fails them on this. They repose in the
general idea that riches contribute to happiness, while
they overlook the fact that happiness has its foundation in character, and that whatever affects that
favourably or unfavourably has a corresponding effect
upon the general well-being of the individual. Now

let us see how the matter stands in regard to the case
we are contemplating. God has supplied to us the
elements of our character in the faculties he has given
us; but the character is formed in the directing and
moulding of these faculties; and this is the appropriate business of education. The great object to be
aimed at in the training of a child is to lead him to
exercise his faculties vigorously and in the right
direction; for it matters not though he should possess
the original powers of a Newton or an Edwards, it is
impossible that he should be either great or good
without becoming used to high intellectual and moral
effort. But do we expect either men or children to
exert themselves without a motive? And do we not
expect that in proportion to the strength of the motive will be the amount of effort? And is it not true
that children who are trained to the expectancy of a
large estate are placed in circumstances that are fitted
to cut the very sinews of even a naturally active and
resolute spirit? The first thought that occurs to them
is that they have no need to submit to the drudgery
of hard labour for their subsistence, and this naturally generates a spirit of idleness; and in the track of
idleness usually follows ignorance, and not unfrequently vice and ultimately ruin. Children of this
class, though they may congratulate themselves, and
be congratulated by others, upon their easy condition,
are generally more to be pitied than the children of
the humblest peasant, who has nothing to give them
but his blessing. I speak with confidence on this
subject, because there is such a long record of facts

spread out before us. There are instances, I acknowledge, in which children who have inherited large estates have been saved from the temptations incident to such a lot, and have made their riches tributary to reputation, usefulness, even true greatness. But the cases are incomparably more numerous in which such children grow up with an incubus upon their faculties which they never throw off, and actually live and die like useless, perhaps noxious, weeds in a luxuriant soil; while much the greater part of those who occupy the highest places of influence and honour in the different walks of society have known from the beginning what it was to depend upon their own efforts, and not unfrequently have struggled up to the eminence they occupy, through barriers which, to an irresolute mind, would have seemed absolutely insurmountable.

I will venture a word of counsel to the opulent business man who is about to make his will. By all means take proper care for your own family: for the wife who has been associated with you in bearing life's burdens; for the children of whom you are the divinely constituted guardian, and some of whom not improbably may be entirely dependent on the provision you make for them; and perhaps for other relatives also, whose necessitous condition may justly entitle them to share in your beneficence. But forget not that there are great objects of religious and public interest to which even a small portion of your wealth would be a most acceptable offering, and say whether it were not better to appropriate a portion to these than to multiply the temptations to your children to a life of ignoble ease, perhaps of profligacy, terminating in ruin. Before you perform this important duty let your judgment, enlightened and unbiassed, have its perfect work; let your conscience be quickened to its highest tone of sensibility; let your mind expand to take in the future as well as the present; and above all, let your spirit be in communion with the God of all counsel and wisdom; and then I will not fear to contemplate the result. I will not fear that you will forget to make provision for perpetuating your good influence after you have fallen asleep.

But business men have much to do in *directing*, as well as in sustaining, our benevolent institutions; their quick discernment, their wisdom, their tact, to the cultivation of which their habits of life are so favourable, are as necessary to give to these institutions their right direction, and secure their legitimate results, as is their money to keep them in vigorous operation. There is a certain kind of practical knowledge which men engaged in active business acquire, but which is not so easily gained by any of the professions, that may be turned to good account in any of the departments of benevolent activity. Hence it will be found, even in respect to those institutions that are more immediately of a religious character, and in which ministers of the Gospel are commonly expected to take the lead, that in their general management great reliance is placed on the common sense and sagacity of our enterprising merchants; and in cases of great difficulty and embarrassment such is the confidence reposed in them that there are few who hesitate to defer to their judgment. Who that has been accustomed to attend the anniversaries of our benevolent institutions does not remember more than one case in which this remark has had a striking exemplification? A great missionary society, for instance—perhaps owing to some unexpected change of circumstances, possibly to a disposition to walk too fast or too far by faith in the liberality of the Church—has become crippled in its movements, and has well-nigh come to a stand, and how it is to recover itself is a problem of which no one is willing to venture a solution. At length an individual, whose voice is perhaps rarely heard in a public meeting, rises and suggests some measure by way of relief, which, though it may involve great effort and liberal contributions, is favourably responded to by one and another, until, after being duly considered and discussed, it is carried by acclamation. And in due time it takes effect, and that noble society, whose fortunes had a little before seemed dubious, is now moving forward again with the majesty of a ship beneath a glorious sky, with every sail filled with a favouring breeze. Now, let us look and see by what instrumentality all this has been accomplished. The man who rose in that meeting, and proposed the measure, and gave the impulse in favour of relief, is at home in a counting-room, and a more busy merchant than he you will rarely meet with. The man who seconded the motion, and those who followed, giving it their cordial support, were all, like the originator, men of business—discreet, liberal, sound-hearted merchants. They determined first what ought to be, and then determined what should be ; and then took care that what they had decreed should come to pass. Had it not been for their timely interposition—their skill in devising, their liberality in executing—who can say how many heathen might have died without the knowledge of a Saviour, who will now walk firmly through the dark valley, knowing in whom they have believed?

I confess that, as I have advanced in this course of thought, my respect, I may say reverence, for business men, and my estimate of the importance which attaches to them as a class, has been growing higher and higher. I cannot but ask myself, what would the government do, what would the Church do, what would our benevolent institutions do, without them? And yet truth constrains me to say that not a small proportion of this class are absorbed in selfish enjoyment, having little sympathy with any of the great interests of humanity. There are thousands who are traitors to the government—not merely by giving their vote for bad rulers, and sacrificing at the shrine of party spirit, but by defrauding the public revenue— sometimes even at the expense of deliberate perjury. There are other thousands who, with their names enrolled on the list of church members, scruple not to take an unjustifiable advantage of their neighbours, or to regard the claims of business as paramount to the claims of religion, or to make the cause of Christ bleed by their habitual insensibility to Divine things. And there are other thousands still, though perhaps they can scarcely be considered as forming a separate class, at whose doors the various objects of Christian bene-

volence and public interest knock and plead in vain ;
who are always haunted and scared by visions of
poverty at home as often as they are asked to contemplate the condition of the destitute abroad, while
for their own personal and selfish gratification they
can be free even to profuseness. From my heart I
pity all such men, and I pity them the more in proportion to their prosperity: for if there is not found a
moth in their treasures, their treasures will certainly
prove a moth to their enjoyment. I blame them not
for their activity in business, but I blame them for
not making it subservient to higher and better interests; I blame them for forgetting that both God
and man have claims upon them which, however they
may repudiate them now, will come with fearful
urgency upon their conscience at another time.

In writing these pages I have not been able to keep
out of my thoughts one living example of a business
man whom I have the privilege to number among
my friends, and whose fine character is worthy alike of
being admired and imitated. I may speak of him
first as I have seen him at home—the head of a lovely
and loving family, where everything moves forward
in obedience to " Heaven's first law;" where there is
a constant ministration and interchange of parental,
and conjugal, and filial affection; where no harsh or
bitter word ever grates upon the ear, and the whole
domestic atmosphere is perfumed with love. But I
think of him now more particularly as a beautiful
illustration of the several topics of which I have been
treating. I cannot say what his politics are, other

than that they are the politics of a true patriot. He loves his country intensely, and considers well all her great interests. He abominates the blustering demagogue, but reverences the enlightened and faithful ruler. He ponders with religious consideration his duties as a citizen, and faithfully does he discharge them, no matter whether his time, or his money, or his influence, be required. He scorns to be the slave of a party, and is as quick to discountenance evil in friends as in foes. And shall I say what he is in his relations to the Church ? Why, in one word, he is an active consistent, devoted member of it. No matter in what circumstances he may be placed, his light never shines dimly even for an hour. In the prayer-meeting, and in other occasional religious exercises, his minister is sure to feel strong when he sees him there. He is always ready, but never obtrusive; always edifying, but never tedious; always discreet, but never time-serving. And he is a Christian in the counting-room as truly as in the lecture-room; a Christian in making a bargain as truly as in hearing a Bible-class, or distributing the elements at the communion. You never hear of his carrying the week into the Sabbath, though he carries much of the Sabbath into the week; and so far from violating that sacred day to return to his family when they are well, he would at least pause and require that it should be an extreme case, before he would consent to patronize any of the Sabbath-desecrating conveyances, even if they were sick. And there is not a more liberal and efficient patron than he of the benevolent institutions of the day. His large pecuniary

means he evidently holds as a steward who must give
an account. His hand is always open to every good
object that solicits his aid. His voice is often heard,
his wisdom is often displayed, when grave matters
connected with the operations of benevolence are discussed. The frosts of nearly threescore and ten winters
have left his powers of mind and body alike untouched.
I might say much more of his excellence and his usefulness, and still leave the picture unfinished. I might
have hesitated to write thus concerning a living man,
but for the conviction I have that, whoever else may
recognize the original, his modesty will keep down all
suspicion.

I wish that this subject might be duly pondered
and applied, especially by our young men of business,
and that, at the very commencement of their career,
they might form the decided Christian purpose to be
true to the government under which they live; true to
the Church of Christ; true to the cause of benevolence; true to all the best interests of both worlds.
Then will they live an honoured and happy life, and
posterity will utter words of reverence and thankfulness around their graves.